Turkey Hunter's Tool Kit: Shooting Savvy

by Jay Langston

Stoeger Publishing Company,   Accokeek, Maryland

Stoeger Publishing
Great Outdoor Books Since 1925

STOEGER PUBLISHING COMPANY
is a division of Benelli U.S.A.

Benelli U.S.A.
Vice President and General Manager:
  Stephen Otway
Director of Brand Marketing and Communications:
  Stephen McKelvain
Vice President of Sales/Strategic Marketing:
  Jack Muety

Stoeger Publishing Company
President: Jeffrey Reh
Publisher: Jay Langston
Managing Editor: Harris J. Andrews
Art Director: Cynthia T. Richardson
Imaging Specialist: William Graves
Copy Editor: Kate Baird
Publishing Assistant: Christine Lawton
Design and Production: Susan K. White

Published by Stoeger Publishing Company
17603 Indian Head Highway, Suite 200
Accokeek, Maryland 20607

BK6471
ISBN:0-883172-38-0
Library of Congress Control Number: 2002105889

Manufactured in the United States of America
Distributed to the book trade and
to the sporting goods trade by:
Stoeger Industries
17603 Indian Head Highway, Suite 200
Accokeek, Maryland 20607
301-283-6300 Fax: 301-283-6986
www.stoegerindustries.com

Contents

Acknowledgments

For my best friend, my wife Jacqueline, who makes it possible for me to have my cake and eat it, too.

My maternal grandparents, Vivian and the late Thomas Rose, sparked my earliest interest in all things wild, and my father fanned the flames. Bob Langston always made time for his young son's passion for the outdoors. Many thanks go to my mother, Margaret, as well, for her patience for things like muddy boots in the house, dove feathers in the dryer and turning her kitchen into an improvised abattoir.

A special thanks goes to my favorite college teacher John Lee, who stood at my career crossroads and showed me how to turn a passion-filled pursuit into a decent living.

My list of friends afield is blessedly long, and to each of these people I owe a debt. Every day spent in pursuit has been a blessing. Reading between the lines of most of what I write about hunting finds Paul Cook, Gene Smith, Andy Turner, Jim Casada or Roger Hook sharing their knowledge and friendship.

Foreword

The book you're holding represents three great things in the lives of American outdoorsmen and -women: good books, good guns and good hunting. They've all come a long way in the last 50 years. The body of literature available to us hunters today continues to amaze me, for just when I think there are no other hook-and-bullet subjects that would really interest me–after a lifetime of reading and a career in outdoor writing and editing–along comes something like the present work.

You've read this before, but when modern turkey hunting broke out, following the magnificent restoration program that saved the birds from almost certain extirpation, there were only a few books about the bird or its hunting. We had, in fact, lost the literature when we almost lost the wild turkey. Check the list today. There are scores of titles, on the bird and its biology, its history and lore, its habitat requirements and management, its hunting and, of course, its proper preparation for the table. We owe a great debt of gratitude to all those who, through the years, have put on paper their knowledge, experiences and expertise concerning our magnificent big-game bird.

None of the effective work of restoring and expanding wild turkey populations across America could have been accomplished without the hunter and his firearms and his freedom to own and use them. We must not lose sight of the fact that America is unique in this regard. Perhaps Gene Denton of Ozark, Arkansas, said it best when he pointed out that our forefathers survived in wild America with the aid of guns, they won our nation's independence with guns, we have successfully defended our way of life in major wars through force of arms, and we pay the bill for wildlife conservation success through hunting license fees and our purchases of sporting firearms and ammunition. Denton's point was that we dare not take for granted our freedom as Americans, our right to own and use firearms or the privileges we enjoy of walking out the door or driving a few miles and going hunting. Amen to all of that.

This book is about guns, yes, and about many of the author's experiences in using a variety of makes and models of firearms, plus bows and arrows, in quest of wild turkeys and white-tailed deer. He knows whereof he speaks. Read him carefully as he describes actions, chokes, loadings and results. He reports the good, the better, the bad and the next-to-useless. Having personally witnessed his persistence at testing and recording various shotgun combinations, I marvel at his patience, his meticulousness and especially at his ability to absorb the pounding that is inherent in bench-testing modern firearms and shotshell loads. It's not for the average shooter.

In *Turkey Hunter's Tool Kit: Shooting Savvy*, the author has told us what worked and what didn't as he chased wild game all around the nation. His accounts of hunts and tactics, both productive and not, impart new knowledge of our sport, while entertaining in fine fashion. What the heck. Just go straight to "The Spectator" *(page 116)* to see what I mean. Enjoy that, then start at the front of the book.

My dad loved cold milk. He'd down a glassful and say, "If the good Lord made anything better than that, He kept it for himself." That's how a lot of us feel about good books, good guns and good hunting. I've got a feeling you're one of us.

—Gene Smith
Retired Editor, *Turkey Call Magazine*

Introduction

Hunting in America was born from a spirit of exploitation begun by Indians who sought to kill wild animals as efficiently as possible to feed a subsistence culture. European settlers joined the American Indian in this subsistence lifestyle, but their more efficient methods and desire to alter the landscape drove many game species to the brink of extinction. Before it was too late, wise hunters saw the handwriting on the wall and became today's heroes of conservation. President Theodore Roosevelt, an avid hunter, put his ideology and reputation on the line as he fought to save remnant wildlife habitat and led the charge to regulate hunting practices. Today, white-tailed deer, elk, mule deer, pronghorn antelope and a host of other game species have flourished to numbers that near or exceed those witnessed by America's earliest pioneers. Of special note is the wild turkey—its numbers depleted to a speculated low of 20,000 by the early 1900s—which has made a spectacular comeback to more than 5 million and growing.

The ideal turkey hunter of the 21st century is a conservationist first and a shooter last. This is exemplified by those hunters who go afield with a specialized shotgun in hand rather than a rifle. Make no mistake, I am not anti-rifle. I find no fault with the Pennsylvania turkey hunter who bags his fall-season bird with a center-fire tack driver. There, as in other locales, turkey hunting with a rifle is a time-honored tradition that predates shotgun hunting and the legal use of calls. Don't mistake the focus of this book on shotguns for elitist arrogance, but consider it instead an honest treatment of what I know. I'll defend a fellow rifleman's choice even though I will continue to pursue this sport with a scattergun.

The self-imposed, short-range limitation set by the use of a shotgun, or bow, speaks volumes about a cadre of sportsmen who spend most of their time afield watching their quarry rather than pulling the trigger. Hunting at its essence is largely about the pursuit. What sets it apart from serious bird watching is one's desire to follow the natural order that was set in motion between predator and prey before man rose to the top of the food chain.

This humble attempt at authorship presents a primer on the use of the "tools of the trade," hence the name "Turkey Hunter's Tool Kit." The suffix "Shooting Savvy" is reference to not only the practical use of a turkey hunter's gun and load, but to their ethical employment as well.

In our fast-paced world some fall into the trap of technology and gadgetry as a shortcut to success. Others, in their rush, often neglect to sharpen their tools. To earn rank in "The Legion" (described in poet Tom Kelly's *The 10th Legion*), one must come to appreciate this most noble of game birds through a studied understanding of the wild turkey's habits and habitats. Along the way to becoming a turkey hunter, woodcraft and calling skills are forged like a Damascus blade: Knowledge of the wild turkey is folded with learned skills and hammered on the anvil of trial and error.

In the pages that follow I hope to give the ardent turkey hunter a fair measure of technical insight that's blended with a strong anecdotal presentation of days spent afield. If you glean just one kernel of information from this book that you put to use next season to bag that long-bearded gobbler, then I'll count my labor as a success.

Call 'em close,

— JAY LANGSTON

I. Shooting Savvy

A hunter's practical understanding of shooting well springs from a combination of study and experience. To help organize my life, I am a list maker. The chapters within this section could be easily viewed as a checklist of sorts that a turkey hunter should consider before pulling the trigger. Mastering the mental aspects of shooting far outweighs the physical. After considering the ideas set forth in the first five chapters, put your knowledge to the test and take heart in the fact that failure is the most profound, long-lasting teacher. Bagging a gobbler with pure, blind luck feels good, but I've learned the greatest lessons from my mistakes. "Missed Opportunities," the title of Chapter 6, plucks success from the ashes of failure.

1. *Take Your Best Shot*

"A wild turkey is a tough animal to bring down, so you've got to pick your shot carefully."

As turkey hunters, we owe it to this great sport to make solid ethical choices throughout the hunt. A wild turkey is a tough animal to bring down, so you've got to pick your shot carefully.

Getting into proper position and being prepared for a shot is a key element of success. Once I've picked a tree for my setup—preferably one wider than my shoulders and taller than my head, for safety's sake—I typically sit with my left knee pointed in the direction from where I expect the bird to approach. I sit with both knees raised and place the gun to my shoulder and the fore-end on my left knee. Sitting in this manner allows me a minimum of movement if the gobbler arrives quietly.

When an opportunity for a shot inside 40 yards presents itself, you should aim for the gobbler's head and neck, which can be tricky at best. A gobbler's vital area—the skull and spinal cord—is pretty small. It's easy to visualize if you compare it to a golf club, about the size of a 5-iron.

WAITING FOR the best moment to shoot is an early lesson learned by all turkey hunters.

When aiming at a gobbler, wait until his neck is fully extended, for the best shot. Avoid body shots at all costs. A gobbler's breast is heavily muscled and tough to penetrate with even the heaviest turkey load. Also, don't shoot a bird in full strut. His neck will be contracted, giving you a much smaller target. Here's a tip. If you want a bird to raise his head, give a loud cluck with a mouth call to get him to snap to attention.

Once that gobbler steps inside gun range, your margin for error gets very narrow. Your adrenaline is pumping and your excitement meter is pegged off the chart. Now's the time to settle down and concentrate on closing the deal.

One of the toughest things to learn is when to make your final adjustments to take a shot on a gobbler. First, have your gun in the ready before the bird even comes into range. Then, adjust your final aim when the bird can't see you make that move. Here's where you use trees or the terrain to cover your movements.

Picture your setup from the bird's perspective. A gobbler's vision must be blocked for you to get away with any kind of movement. Move at the wrong time and the game's over. Wait to move your gun until his head goes behind a tree. Remember, the obstruction has to be nearer to the bird than to your position, to be effective. The closer the tree is to the bird, the wider the area of his vision that is obstructed.

If a strutting bird comes in from your blind side, here's another trick: Wait until he turns away and his fan blocks his view. Cheek the gun and wait for him to turn around or come out of strut, and then take the shot.

Keep these tips in mind and you'll up your chances for success when it's time to pull the trigger on a long-bearded gobbler.

A WILD TURKEY'S skull and neck bones make a small target.

2. The Confidence Factor

Many years ago, when I devoted my time to making a living in sales, a book written by Napoleon Hill, *Think and Grow Rich*, was popular for putting salesmen in the right frame of mind. Another use of positive mental imagery is when Olympic athletes are in trancelike thought devoted to imagining their success. More specifically, Olympic shooters spend a tremendous amount of time looking at targets–not shooting–just watching. Adding a few mental exercises to your overall turkey hunting skills can lead to increased success at those moments when the adrenaline is high as a gobbler approaches your setup.

It's been said over and over that patience is the biggest factor in a turkey hunter's success. There's a lot of truth to this philosophy, but before a turkey hunter can achieve the patience of a predator, he must have confidence in several areas–calling skills, woodsmanship, shooting ability, gun performance, etc.

A shining example is a hunt in April 1996 that should have ended much differently. I was hunting with Harold Knight, co-owner of Knight and Hale Game Calls, near his home in Cadiz, Kentucky. Well before daylight on the last morning of a three-day hunt, Harold picked me up in his woods-scarred Blazer and drove a short distance to a ridge where he had located a gobbler. As we drove the last 200 yards, Harold killed his headlights and navigated by feel up the spine of a rocky, hardwood ridge. A quiet 10-minute hike downwind of where the tom was supposed to be put us where Harold thought we should listen for the first gobbles of the morning.

As it soon turned out, the first longbeard we had heard that morning was on another ridge a

PRACTICE SIGHTING your gun in dimly lit woods to get ready for the real thing.

half-mile away. The birds Harold was looking for hadn't sounded off after a few minutes, so he owl-hooted and got the attention of the turkey he was searching for—and a nearby whitetail. The problem was that we had walked directly underneath the tom on his roost, probably spooking him in the process. Adding to our dilemma was the snorting deer that knew something questionable was afoot. Luckily we had the wind in our favor, so the deer soon lost interest, but not before sounding the alarm. Trying to call a spooked gobbler raises the odds in the bird's favor tenfold. By all accounts, I normally would have walked away from this situation and moved in on the first tom that was gobbling his brains out a few hundred yards away.

But Harold was determined to give the bird a try. So we moved in a few yards and set up and called. When the bird answered, Harold shifted our position again. As Harold increased his calling, the tom seemed to warm up to the lascivious invitations of romance. To add to the realism of the setup, the veteran woodsman whispered to me that he would back off and call from various spots behind where I was sitting.

Several minutes later, a jake sailed from his roost to the bench below me and began his raucous yelping. The combination of Harold's calls and the jake's unwanted competition was too much for the longbeard. He sailed down and marched toward me, gobbling every few steps. Moments later, a 2-ounce Remington Duplex load of Nos. 4 and 6 shot anchored the 21-pound tom.

Confidence, mostly Harold's, is what put that longbeard in front of my Remington 11-87 that morning. This simple lesson is one that's difficult to apply for most hunters. Hunters walk away from killable birds every season because their confidence is lacking. National Wild Turkey Federation treasurer Earl Groves pounded home the point in his features on "Confidence

THE AUTHOR and Harold Knight, right, replay a successful hunt.

Shooting Tips

- Know what a turkey looks like over the barrel of your shotgun. You're probably thinking this sounds oversimplified, but in practice, it will enable you to make a good shot.
- In dimly lit woods while wearing a head net, squeeze one eye shut and aim your sights at a turkey head-sized target.
- If your eye remains focused on the front bead or sight—where it's supposed to be—the target will be a blur.
- If you make the mistake of focusing on the turkey when you're taking the slack out of a trigger, there's a good chance you will raise your face off the comb of the stock and shoot over the bird.
- The mental exercise is learning how to focus your eyes on your sights while focusing your mind on the bird's vitals. Practice this technique at various distances before the season starts and your accuracy with a tight-choked shotgun will improve measurably.

Calling," in the January and March 1995 issues of *Turkey Call* magazine. Practice the different parts of your hunting repertoire, and confidence in your overall turkey hunting abilities will rise.

11

3. The Importance of Range Estimation

Bowhunting for deer and shotgunning wild turkeys share many similar attributes of short-range big game hunting pursuits. One is the chance to intimately learn the quarry hunted, through close observation. On the other hand, there's the certainty that any mistakes made on the hunter's part spell trouble if your intentions are more than just observing a bouncing whitetail's flag or watching how adept wild turkeys are at flying. With either pursuit, range estimation is one of the biggest areas where miscues turn into missed opportunities.

The guns and loads available today for turkey hunting translate into a 40-yard-and-less pursuit. Estimating when a gobbler is within range is easy, if you practice.

Range estimation is a skill that must be learned through repetitive practice. A lot of novice turkey hunters do their homework—practice calling, pattern their guns and outfit themselves in full camo—only to go afield without a skill that is equally important.

It has been proven in military field tests that the average person estimates range with a probable error of 30 percent. Even with intense training, visual range estimation gets no better than 15 percent of actual distance.

If the average untrained person has a 30 per-

PRESEASON RANGE estimation practice will pay off when your adrenaline is high.

cent-error handicap, it's a pretty sure bet that a lot of turkey hunters go afield ill prepared.

Borrowing a tool from the bowhunting fraternity is the simplest way to accurately judge distance. Several rangefinding devices are available to help you estimate distance. I've used a Ranging 50/2 Mini Rangefinder for bowhunting and turkey hunting for more than a decade and like its compactness and light weight. Ranging also offers a TRL 75 model that accurately measures distance from 10 to 75 yards. These devices use a system of mirrors to produce split images of an object. Look at the images through the viewfinder, adjust the distance indication knob until the images become a single image, then read the distance indicated.

Another device I tested several bow seasons ago was Brunton's Laser70 Rangefinder. This device is about the size of a bologna sandwich, weighs less than 10 ounces and can be worked with one hand. It is accurate to within one yard between five and 70 yards. In the years since, Brunton discontinued this model of rangefinder. DME Rangefinders in McKewen, Tennessee, was Brunton's original supplier and has since continued manufacturing under its own name.

When a gobbler is coming to your call is obviously not the time to try out a rangefinder. If you go the route of using a rangefinder, don't make the mistake of trying it out the first time the morning you go turkey hunting. A little practice at home will go a long way toward later success.

Once you're in the woods and setting up to call in a longbeard, find various landmarks, trees, rocks, etc., to note distance when you first set up. By the time a tom strolls within range, you should be ready to shoot rather than squinting through a peephole.

Accurate range estimation could help you in another way as well. I've found that there's a threshold at about 25 yards where mistakes, usually hunter movement, seem to be more critical than when a gobbler is beyond this distance. When a bird approaches this "hyper zone," practically any hunter movement can spell disaster. On several occasions I've watched birds within gun range, but beyond 25 yards, hesitate when they saw something they didn't like and often calm back down if they didn't see something else to confirm their fears. Inside 25 yards, a gobbler's best judgment is full retreat if he becomes suspicious. This isn't a hard-and-fast rule, but it's something to consider when afield.

A little practice will make you a better turkey hunter, so take the opportunity now to sharpen your range-estimation skills before the next hunting season rolls around.

RANGING RANGEFINDER MODEL 75 is the smallest and lightest unit sold. Primarily used for medium range applications where targets will be closer than 75 yards/meters.

THE DME LASER RANGEFINDER is small, light and highly portable and has in-view display of distance. It features a unique audible target indicator that can be turned off for totally silent operation.

Ranging Tips

There's another method that works well if you don't choose to use a rangefinder.

- Have a partner place a turkey decoy at an unknown distance in the woods, sit down and guess the yardage.
- Vary the terrain, lighting conditions, and brush to present true hunting situations.
- Remember to sit down to estimate range because things look different at turkey-eye-level compared to a human's normal vantage point.
- Several National Wild Turkey Federation chapters have incorporated this game into their JAKES youth events with a lot of success.

4. Obstacles to Good Shooting

Some turkey hunters are under the mistaken impression that two ounces of shot will smash cleanly through most anything and kill a gobbler. But at best, firing through a hazard is an unsure proposition.

I've had good fortune the past several seasons because I've waited for a clear shot. Other times, because of some hazard between the bird and me, I've passed up shots and left the woods empty handed despite being tempted by a gobbling tom within easy gun range. A small twig, sapling or vine all seem like small obstacles, but they can wreck a shot pattern and turn a killing shot into a miss, or worse, a crippling shot.

A load of lead shot hitting briars or small saplings is much like a train wreck. When pellets strike a small branch or weed, they ricochet, slow down and the pellets behind plow into the back of the forward shot, causing both to go off course.

Another thing that happens to lead shot when it strikes an obstacle is that the individual pellets get misshapen and take on the flight characteristics of a Phil Neikro knuckleball. All that banging and bouncing causes the shot to scatter.

Two factors play significant roles in shot pattern disruption. First, the distance between the obstruction and the gobbler will determine the gaps in the pattern. For instance, if the obstruction is at 10 yards and the bird is at 35, the pattern will be more disrupted than if the obstruction is only a few feet from the tom. The farther shot has to travel to its target after running into interference, the larger the gaps grow within the pattern. Second, the size and density of the hazard determine the havoc played on the pattern. The bigger the obstruction is, the more pellets will strike it. And, the harder the obstruction, the more severely the pellets will be deformed, causing them to fly even more erratically.

A few years ago, I ran into a couple of situations where paying attention to what lay between the muzzle and the turkey meant the difference between a bird bagged and a bird lost.

The weekend of Georgia's opener, I hunted with a friend,

THE SHOT ABSORBED by this 1½-inch sapling saved an Illinois gobler from becoming a hunter's trophy.

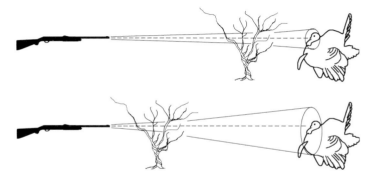

THE DISTANCE between an obstacle, such as vines, and the bird influences shot dispersion.

Richard Wansley, and we had worked four young gobblers to a hog wire fence. The birds gobbled at our calling and strutted back and forth behind the fence 70 yards in front of us. Finally, one of the jakes came around the fence and strode to within a few yards of us. Richard's son, Jordan, drew a bead and hammered the obliging jake.

The next morning, Richard and I went back to the same spot, but set up on the side of the fence where we first saw the jakes the evening before. But when the birds flew down, they landed on the side of the fence opposite us.

Richard and I called to the three jakes and they worked their way toward us. I picked a gap in the four-by-four-inch mesh and waited for a bird to get lined up. I wanted the bird as close to the fence as possible, to minimize the effect of pattern dispersal after striking the fence. I didn't have long to wait. One of the hefty jakes stepped into my window of opportunity and I dropped him. Since the muzzle was only 10 feet from the fence, the pattern dispersal was minimal and the results were entirely predictable.

On another occasion that same season, I hunted with World Turkey Calling Champ Steve Stoltz in Illinois at Heartland Lodge. Steve and I both connected on longbeards the first morning out, so I spent the rest of the hunt carrying a still camera.

I was crossing a cow pasture with Mark Drury and his brother, Terry, when we heard a distant gobble from the bottom of a steep draw. Terry was the appointed shooter, so he set up, with Mark backing him. I took up the rear to catch the bird on camera. When he got within range, I could just make out the tip of his fan. He strutted and gobbled to every call. When the bird crossed the 30-yard mark, Terry felt he had an open shot and fired. The problem was that a 1½-inch-diameter sapling stood in the way. Several pellets struck the tree, saving the tremendous bird to gobble another day. Well, two days.

Two days later, M.A.D. Calls staff member Tad Brown called the bird to the same spot and killed it. The heavyweight bird carried 1½-inch spurs and a rope-like beard–a trophy in any turkey hunter's estimation.

It's normal to overlook or ignore the presence of a sapling at 20 yards when you are focusing either on your gun sights or a bird standing 35 yards away. Scopes can aid you in seeing obstructions between you and your target.

Bottom line, pay attention to the little things that could block your success and it can make all the difference in the world.

WAITING for a clear shot is the best bet.

5. On Target:
Point of Aim/Point of Impact

"After you've found a load that patterns well, one that will put more than 100 pellets in a 10-inch circle at 40 yards, it's time to do some fine tuning."

You've spent countless hours getting ready for turkey season. You've scouted a great location with plenty of gobblers.

But what about your turkey gun?

There are some very important aspects of shooting a turkey gun accurately that need your attention before the season rolls around. After you've found a load that patterns well, one that will put more than 100 pellets in a 10-inch circle at 40 yards, it's time to do some fine tuning.

When you're shooting a tight-patterning shotgun at a small target–such as a gobbler's head and neck–you have to be sure the core of the load is hitting precisely where you aim. As in shooting a rifle, changing loads from one brand to the next can change the point of impact downrange. Switching choke tubes can change point of impact, too. Here are a few tips to keep in mind:

When sighting-in, use a steady rest.

Wear your hunting clothes, to make sure the gun fits you in practice the same way it does in the field.

FITTING A LOW-POWER scope can help adjust your gun's point of aim.

A 10-INCH TARGET works well for determining pattern density, but a larger target is needed to learn point of impact.

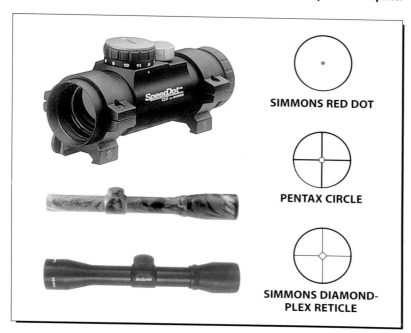

SIMMONS RED DOT

PENTAX CIRCLE

SIMMONS DIAMOND-PLEX RETICLE

Try a few shots from a sitting position with the gun propped on your knee, to make sure your eye–your rear sight–is lining up the same as it did from the shooting bench.

If your turkey gun has bead sights, make sure you go through a mental checklist each time you shoot:

• Hold your face tight to the stock every time.

• Make sure the beads are in perfect alignment.

• Keep your shooting eye focused on the front sight, which should slightly blur the target.

What if your shotgun doesn't center the pattern where you're aiming? That's when adjustable rifle-type sights come in handy. There are several models available that will clamp onto your existing shotgun barrel rib, or you can have

a gunsmith install a set. When you've got them in place, it's a simple matter of fine-tuning the adjustments to get everything lined up.

Another option is a low-powered scope. A zero to 3X magnification will work the best. Some scopes have standard cross hairs, while others offer various range-finding reticles. Either diamond-shaped or circular, the center of the reticle covers a specified area, which corresponds to different measurements at different ranges. With practice, you can gauge the range to a gobbler by comparing the reticle's center area to a part of the bird's body, such as the distance from the top of his head to his beard. Simmons, Pentax, Bushnell and Burris scopes have proven top performers on my turkey guns over the years. Whichever

model you choose, make sure the eye relief is long enough to keep your face away from the rear of the scope.

Although I've been lucky, I have seen a few turkey hunters who got too close to their scopes and got some nasty cuts when the scope came back in recoil.

Over the past few seasons, I've had success with "dot" scopes, ones that use a simple dot as the aiming point. I've had equal success with Simmons, Aimpoint and Burris models.

It's simple to adjust the dot to cover the center of your shot pattern. And, it's easier to keep your gun on target, even in odd shooting positions. A real big advantage is that your sights and your target are in perfect focus at the same time.

Once you get accustomed to shooting with a scope, you'll learn what I have: Getting lined up on a cagey old gobbler is every bit as fast as shooting with standard bead sights.

6. Missed Opportunities

I recall a conversation a few years ago with a coworker who said he had never missed a turkey. No, he wasn't a rookie who had been lucky a couple of times in a row. This guy was an honest-to-goodness turkey slayer with more beards to his credit than you could fit in a big shoebox.

"Nope, never missed," he declared.

"Never?" I quizzed.

I had already spilled my guts about missing a gobbler the previous spring, and he didn't miss the opportunity to toss some salt on the wound. He told wonderful tales that were sure to be chiseled in granite at the Turkey Shooters Hall of Fame.

He went on about this and that and how his trusty turkey thumper would throw such a thick pattern that no turkey alive would ever stand a chance if it put a toe across the 40-yard mark.

Mashed the salt in good and dosed me again for good measure.

I peered from behind an upturned coffee mug that concealed my grin. Not that I'm superstitious or believe in jinxes, but I had the future flash before my eyes that day. I didn't want to spoil his day, so I just kept my mouth shut. Guess what happened to Ole Deadeye the next spring? Yup. Broke his streak, in front of witnesses, on camera, no less. Spend enough time staring down a shotgun barrel at gobblers' heads and you will eventually miss.

One of the most common reasons turkey hunters miss is that they get enthralled by the spectacle, or get in an awkward position and

LIFTING THE cheek off the stock is the leading reason for misses.

18

pull their cheek off the stock. Gun goes off . . . shot goes high . . . turkey runs or flies away . . . end of story!

Enough has been said lately about putting scopes on turkey guns. Another alternative is to make sure your turkey gun has adjustable sights, which are better than standard bead sights, for a couple of reasons.

Twisted logic

Turkey guns don't always shoot where they're aimed. Sometimes they come slightly off from the factory. Perhaps a bit of rough handling bent the barrel–it doesn't take much to bend a shotgun barrel. I laid a Remington 870 12-gauge in the bottom of a johnboat one

morning on the way to the duck blind. One of my friend's retrievers stepped on the gun and bent the barrel enough to throw the pattern off by two feet. You couldn't see the bend, but it was there all right. Installing adjustable sights might help remedy a gun that won't shoot where you are looking.

Peek-a-boo

Yet another reason we miss is that we don't always know when to stop turkey "hunting" and start turkey "shooting," which is an easy mistake to make. I have been as guilty as the next person, even though I know better. The scenario plays out something like this:

The gobbler struts into view well out of range while I admire the show. Call a little more and he eventually walks within range. About this time I've got target acquisition . . . target locked . . .tone . . . Fire!

With all the adrenaline and fanfare, it's easy to focus on the wrong thing–the turkey. If you are not focused on the front sight of your gun, which puts the turkey out of focus,

LETTING A GOBBLER walk away is better than rushing a risky shot.

it's coincidental that the shot goes where you want it. Rifle-type sights or the newer fiber optic models do a better job of focusing your attention on what's most important: When to quit hunting and start shooting.

Loaded questions
Turkey loads don't always shoot where they're aimed. Gun writers have waxed evangelistic about re-sighting rifles when switching loads. The same holds true for tight-shooting turkey guns.

Although different ammo can shoot to different points-of-aim at varying distances, it's more critical inside 20 yards, when patterns tend to be ultratight. Again, adjustable sights help get you back on target.

The dark side
Too many times to count, I've had turkeys fly, run and walk into my setups so early that the cardinals hadn't even started stirring. Early encounters, rainy days, thick foliage or a combination make for poor shooting light. That's when one of the fiberoptic sights is worth its weight in gold.

Compromising positions
I've had to shoot at turkeys in more weird positions than you could find in the Kama Sutra (for you married folks out there). A simple bead sight may not help you keep on target when that gobbler walks up from behind and to the side where you normally shoulder the gun. Suddenly you're trying to become ambidextrous. A more refined sighting device, such as rifle-type sights or a "dot" sight might help you stay on target.

Options abound
As turkey guns have become more refined, a few firearms manufacturers have added rifle sights to better fit a turkey hunter's needs. Many factory models now reach the market with fiber-optic sights. If your favorite shotgun is without and you're ready to do something about it, several

models of sights are available as aftermarket add-ons.

Weaver, the original scope company that went away and came back under the Blount flag, offered the granddaddy of today's fiber-optic shotgun sights. No longer made, these sights were an all-metal tube with an orange light-gathering insert. The sights attach to the shotgun's rib and are right-and-left adjustable. I found two of these sights in a dusty attic several years ago and feel lucky to have them. I'd love to have a hundred of them. They were the Cadillac of sights.

Today, TRUGLO, HiViz, Williams and others offer add-on sights for shotguns. Some are clamp-on models, while others use magnets or adhesive tape to hold them in place, which allows their use without a trip to the gunsmith. If you have no fear and a drill, Carlson's offers high-visibility front and mid-rib sights, along with a handy tool for centering drill bits on ventilated ribs. Carlson's sells the correct size drill bits and taps, too. Brownell's also offers a host of after-market shotgun sights.

If you are ready to upgrade your turkey gun, give one of these options a try. It just may make the difference the next time you flip the safety off and start squeezing the slack out of your trigger.

A SCOPE will make ackward shots possible.

II. *Tools of the Trade*

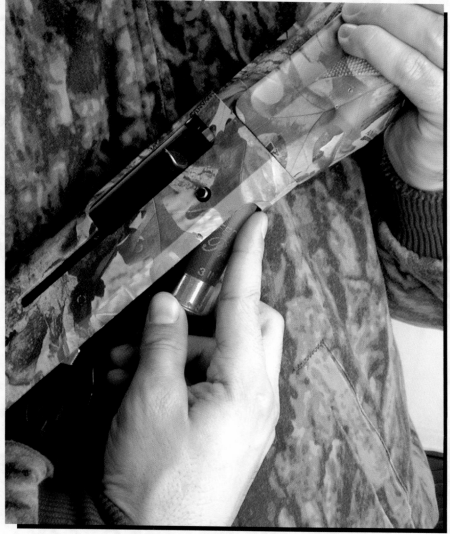

The 12-gauge shotgun has become the standard by which all other bore diameters are measured in regards to use for turkey hunting. The following section takes the reader down the path traveled in shotgun specifications for turkey hunting.

Turkey hunters wishing to set an edge by lugging around a 10 gauge can gain a slight edge, but at a cost. Chapter 8 chronicles my experience with the sledgehammer 10 gauge.

Chapter 9 takes a look at the lighter side of turkey hunting. The 20 gauge offers a reliable lightweight gun for those willing to rely more on their calling skill than a gun that will reach a gobbler in the next zip code.

7. Evolution of The Turkey Gun

Over the past quarter-century, wild turkey populations have grown tremendously, creating more opportunities for hunters to pursue these noble creatures. As the number of hunters grew in response to this new opportunity, gun manufacturers raced to fill the specialized equipment niche that was created.

For many turkey hunters the gun of choice was a full-choked 12-gauge. Many of these fixed-choke models were waterfowl sporters with 30- to 36-inch barrels. By the late 1980s, however, several gun companies began to cut their shotgun barrel lengths to accommodate turkey hunters' needs for easy-to-aim guns in tight brush. Camouflaged shotguns also came into vogue, to

THESE OLD TIME turkey hunters in Arkansas are armed with both rifles and shotguns.

SAVAGE 24 F COMBINATION RIFLE/SHOTGUN

conceal shiny metal from wary gobbler eyes.

One of the earliest firearms dedicated to turkey hunting was the Savage Model 24 combination gun. Savage began production in 1950 with a .22 rimfire rifle over a .410 shotgun; it later evolved into the Model 24 F, which was labeled the Predator version, chambered in .22 LR, .22 Hornet, .222 Remington, .223 Remington, or .30-30 caliber over 12 or 20 gauge. The 24-inch shotgun barrels were chambered in 3-inch magnum. The Model 24 F added a "T" (turkey) version chambered in .22 Hornet or .223 Remington caliber over 12 gauge. The Model 24 T featured rifle sights and a camouflaged Rynite stock and forearm. Unfortunately, the Savage Model 24 F-T met with limited sales and was discontinued in 1989.

Prior to 1987, few, if any, firearms manufacturers offered shotguns specifically designed for turkey hunting that fit today's ideal: short barrel, accepting extended extra-full choke tubes, camo finish, fitted for a sling, rifle sights, etc.

Working in cooperation with gun manufacturers, a team of experienced turkey hunters on the National Wild Turkey Federation (NWTF) national staff shared design ideas that produced shotguns offering features that work well in hunting situations. These men also shared their expertise on gun designs that would command premium prices in the fund-raising banquet arena. Many of the early guns were embellished with engraved wild turkey scenes created by NWTF CEO Rob Keck.

Through the hard work of NWTF volunteers and the organization's explosive growth, many firearms manufacturers have been willing to pay a premium for the NWTF seal of approval through "trade gun" agreements. Several newer turkey gun variations have even been developed as a result of past NWTF gun programs. The resulting dollars raised through NWTF gun sales have benefited wild turkey restoration and management across the country.

A flurry of wildcat cartridges is often developed on the heels of any new factory centerfire cartridge that is developed. Once the initial research and development creates a new cartridge, it paves the way for shooting enthusiasts to tinker with new variations based on the parent cartridge case. A similar occurrence took place when Winchester Arms developed the Win Choke interchangeable choke tube system. Gunsmiths around the country began tinkering with the new technology to create and improve new chokes for various shooting applications. One of the largest uses in after-market choke tubes is for turkey hunters wanting to shoot tight patterns with relatively large payloads. One of the earliest companies specializing in choke tubes was Nu-Line Guns, in Harvester, Missouri. I recall sending a 12-gauge Remington 870 barrel to Nu-Line in the mid-1980s to be cut to 21½ inches, threaded, and a .670 choke tube installed. The only threading equipment Nu-Line Guns had at the time was for Winchester's proprietary Winchokes, so I wound up with a Remington that would only accept Winchester choke tubes. It was an unusual match, but one that has accounted for its fair share of turkeys in the years since. Today, there are nearly two dozen companies offering aftermarket choke tubes for turkey hunting, and nearly any modern turkey shotgun is able to accommodate them.

Another significant development was the advent of the 3½-inch 12-gauge shotgun and

NATIONAL WILD TURKEY FEDERATION LIMITED EDITIONS

Manufacturer	Model	Quantity	Year
Navy Arms	Black Powder 12-ga.	500	1983
Winchester	Model 23	300	1985
Browning	BPS 12-ga.	500	1986
American Arms	SxS 10-ga. 3 1/2 in.	150	1987
Winchester	Model 1300 Win-Cam 12-ga.	500	1987/88
Winchester	Model 1300 12-ga. Trade Gun	-	-
Beretta	Model A-303 12-ga.	500	1988/89
Winchester	Model 1300 Win-Cam 12-ga.	500	1989
Winchester	Model 1300 12-ga. Trade Gun	-	1989
Browning	Model A5 12-ga.	500	1990
Mossberg	Model 835 12-ga. Auction	500	1991
Mossberg	Model 835 Trade Gun	-	1991-97
Remington	Model 11-87 12-ga. Auction	500	1992
Remington	Model 11-87 12-ga. Trade Gun	-	-
Winchester	Model 1300 12-ga. Auction	500	1993
New England Firearms	S.S. 20-ga. Auction	-	-
New England Firearms	S.S. 10-ga. Trade Gun	-	-
New England Firearms	S.S. 10-ga. Auction	-	-
Mossberg	Model 9200 12-ga. Gun of the Year	500	1994
New England Firearms	20-ga. Topper Model JAKES Gun	-	1994
Franchi (American Arms)	12-ga. Semi-Auto	600	1995
Fausti (American Arms)	12-ga. O/U	780	1996
Fausti (American Arms)	12-ga. O/U	900	1997
New England Firearms	20-ga. Topper Model JAKES Gun	-	1997
Remington	Model 870 12-ga.	1,200	1998
Remington	Model 870 20-ga. JAKES Gun	-	1998
Remington	Model 870 12-ga. Trade Gun	-	1998
Remington	Model 11-87 12-ga. Trade Gun	-	1998
Remington	Model 11-87 20-ga. Trade Gun	-	1998
Remington	Model SP-10 10-ga. Trade Gun	-	1998
Beretta	Model ES-100 12-ga. Mossy Oak Trade Gun	-	1999
Beretta	Model Realtree AL390 12-ga.	-	1999
Beretta	Model AL390 12-ga. Black Synthetic	-	1999
Beretta	Model AL390 20-ga. Youth	-	1999
Ithaca	Model 37 Turkeyslayer	-	2000
Browning	BPS 12-ga.	-	2001
Winchester	Super X-2 12-ga.	-	2002

THE MOST recent innovation in turkey hunting is tungsten-nickel shot.

shell. Mossberg is credited with developing the first shotgun for the 3½-inch magnum, in the late 1980s. They toyed with the idea of resurrecting the 10-gauge in their Model 500 shotgun to answer the dilemmas faced with shooting steel shot at waterfowl. Key personnel at Mossberg learned that Federal Cartridge and Browning had discussed the idea of a 3½-inch shell and gun to shoot the magnum loading, but Browning opted for the 10-gauge instead, to solve the woes of shooting steel. When Mossberg's engineers learned of this decision, they went to the drawing board and developed the 835 Ulti-Mag. An agreement with Federal to supply the 3½-inch ammo set the wheels in motion for producing this successful gun/load marriage. A short time later, 3½-inch turkey loads were developed for the 12-gauge, and a new era in turkey guns was born.

Several shotgun manufacturers have followed suit by offering 3½-inch chambered 12-gauge guns. Benelli USA introduced the first successful 3½-inch 12-gauge semi-auto

with its Super Black Eagle, which is recognized as the top of its class for waterfowling and turkey hunting in the super magnum 12-gauge class. Remington first added their Model 870 Super Magnum pump-action shotgun to their lineup, which was soon followed by a semi-auto version 11-87 in 2000.

Another resurrection of sorts is worthy of mention, as it relates to turkey gun evolution. Black powder enthusiasts have long been able to tailor loads for turkey hunting, but over the last few years, a few gun companies have added state-of-the-art technology to their guns. Modern Muzzle Loading developed a 12-gauge barrel for their MK-95 interchangeable-barrel in-line guns. These sweet-shooting guns are fitted with screw-in choke tubes that measure .660,

and the combination produces excellent results on turkeys. Using wads from modern shotshells and copper-plated shot in front of 100 grains of Pyrodex, these guns are magnums in their own right. At the 40-yard line, they can compete with the best magnum turkey loads on the market.

NWTF Turkey Guns

To follow the progress and change in turkey hunting arms, one might take a glance at the list of shotguns selected by the NWTF as their Guns of the Year, as well as NWTF-sanctioned trade guns. These guns often led to innovations that have become standards for the turkey gun. Over the years, certain models were selected for reasons beyond their functional use. Instead of choosing the most popular turkey gun models in some years, NWTF management opted instead to anoint guns that offered a certain price level that would yield the most return through sales in fundraising banquets. Between 1995 and 1997, three American Arms models sank below the quality levels of NWTF guns before or since.

MOSSBERG 835 ULTI-MAG PUMP SHOTGUN

BENELLI SUPER BLACK EAGLE

8. Are Bigger Bores Better?

A REMINGTON SP-10 and Nitro
3-ounce load clobbered this
gobbler in 2001.

Conversations between turkey hunters often turn to their favorite guns and loads to pursue these wily birds. Many times I've heard hunters proudly state their turkey slayer can dot a bird's eye well past 40 paces. The methods they pursue to put a tight pattern of their favorite turkey load on their target is to shoot either 1¾-ounce high-velocity or 2-ounce turkey loads from a 12-gauge. Some even choose to step up in bore size to 10-gauge. I've heard debates grow long and loud as to which magnum bore size is best for dispatching a gobbler.

Although somewhat limited, I have managed to bag a few toms with the 10-gauge mag-nums over the years. Looking back at my hunting journal, I find that much of my 1995 season was spent with a Remington SP-10 in my hands. In reality, it probably spent most of its time slung across my shoulder, the signif-icance of which I'll return to later.

The first gobbler I set up on while toting the magnum 10-

gauge was on the opening day of Alabama's spring season. I was hunting on the Greenway Sportsman's Club, near Union Springs. Before daylight, Phillip Green, now deceased, dropped me off on a lonely blacktop road where an abandoned railroad bed crossed. After a half-mile walk, I stopped to listen for a gobbler to ring in the new season. Two longbeards greeted the day in a 20-year-old pine plantation adjacent to the old rail bed. I dropped off the rail bed and followed an old power line right-of-way that angled uphill, behind the roosted birds.

At daylight, I started a conversation that convinced one of the longbeards to stroll up the hill for a visit. I remember well the sensation that every veteran turkey hunter knows: It's that twang of uncertainty when a gobbler flies from his roost and gobbles when he hits the ground. Once the bird is on the ground, it's hard to tell if the bird is moving in your direction or away, since his gobbles are more muffled at ground level than when he's singing on the limb.

Some soft purrs, clucks and yelps on a battle-scarred H.S. Strut slate pulled the tom a few yards up the hill, his gobbles a little clearer than when he first hit the ground. He was on his way! At 7:10 a.m., the longbeard strutted to the other side of the narrow opening. I could see the top of his fan just above the tops of the thigh-high green winter wheat 20 yards away. I centered the bead on his fan tips and clucked once with a mouth call. Fan went down and head came up. The big 10-gauge roared, parting the green wheat like Moses parted the Red Sea. The two-year-old gobbler carried a 9½-inch beard and weighed two ounces shy of 18 pounds.

While gathering information for another article that season, a few things stick in my mind from the experience. One aspect is that the lighter 2¼-ounce loads patterned nearly twice as well as the 2½- and 3-ounce Nitro loads. Too much of a good thing, indeed.

The second thing was the recoil. I haven't suffered any adverse reactions yet. (My old friends will swear that I was this way before absorbing between 4,000 and 5,000 turkey loads over the last 10 years.) I won't hesitate to

THIS 1995 South Carolina tom fell to a 3-ounce Nitro duplex 10-gauge load.

say, though, that I prefer shooting guns and loads that don't leave me feeling like I've boxed 10 rounds with George Foreman.

Another thing I remember from that season was the weight of the gun itself. Lugging that SP-10, or any other 10-gauge for that matter, will wear down anyone after carrying it for several miles all day in rough terrain. By comparison, toting a 12-gauge, or 20-gauge is pleasant when you compare the weight differences. Other turkey guns on the market today will weigh two to three pounds less than the big 10s.

By now you've probably got the notion that I don't like 10-gauge guns. Personally, I know that they can be reliable performers on turkeys, but at what cost? The added weight of these guns alone is enough to push me toward a lighter-weight gun. I don't need to get hammered by recoil when patterning the big 10s to remind me that I'm having fun, either.

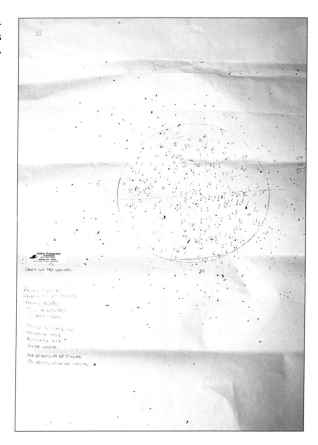

A NITRO Tri-plex 3-ounce 10-gauge load put 312 pellets inside a 10-inch circle.

I'll make a prediction that the turkey hunting industry will see a surge in the other direction in coming years. More veteran turkey hunters will find pleasure in carrying a finely tuned 20-gauge turkey gun and working birds a bit closer before pulling the trigger. One thing's for sure, it takes more hunting skill and patience to bring a bird into 30 yards and live by the self-imposed limits of a shorter-range gun. Add a hefty number of youth and women entering the sport and it is easy to see the market expanding in the future for 20-gauge turkey guns and loads.

In 2000, I shared some of my opinions about the mighty 10-gauge in a turkey gun article in *Turkey Call* magazine. One thing is for sure, turkey hunters are quick to share their opinions about their favorite guns. I had several readers agree with my assertion that a 12-gauge is more than adequate turkey medicine. However, I vividly recall one NWTF member who thought I had lost my mind because I had a rather low opinion of 10-gauge guns. This guy was so upset that I had maligned the mighty 10-gauge that he wrote me, wrote my boss and even wrote a complaint letter to an NWTF board member. I was afraid he was going to tell my mom, so I agreed to try turkey hunting with a 10-gauge again just to get this guy off my back.

When it comes to 10-gauge turkey guns, the list is rather short. It was a no-brainer to call Linda Powell, the manager of press relations at Remington, and ask her if she would lend me an SP-10 for turkey season. She also agreed to let me ship the gun to Ray Filogomo, at Nitro Company, in Gilboa, New York, for fine tuning, so I could get the best possible results.

When the green box arrived on my desk a few weeks later, there was also a smaller package that contained a note, a tattered patterning target and 10 rounds of ammo. I got quite a surprise when I unfolded the target, which looked as if someone had shot the target more than once with a heavy turkey load at close range. It had an unbelievable 312 pellet holes inside a 10-inch circle. Ray's note said the target was fired at 40 yards. The impressive pat-

tern was the result of a Nitro Triplex load consisting of three crushing ounces of No. 4s, No. 5s and No. 7 1/2 shot. The gun was fitted with a Rhino .685 choke. A few days later, I fired a few rounds and got similar results. All that remained was to wait for turkey season to open to put the big 10 to the test.

We had been watching a pair of mature gobblers for a month leading up to the 2001 turkey season. Every few days, a third gobbler or a few jakes would join a pair of gobblers that always traveled together. It was easy to pick the pair out of a lineup: One gobbler was huge by South Carolina standards and the other tom was a mature, beardless miniature. They reminded me of a cartoon bulldog and his Chihuahua sidekick.

Three days into the season, a fellow club member tagged the bigger 22-pound brute and the whole flock moved out of the area for a few days. A week later, the beardless tom returned to his normal habits and I set my plan. I eased through a young pine plantation to the head of a little wooded drain. I tiptoed the last few yards through dried sweetgum leaves, but at the first crunch, two toms gobbled from their dark perch at the noise below. I had no choice but to stake my decoys a few feet away and sit down pronto.

After things settled down a bit and it began to get light in the east, I made a few tree yelps with a mouth call. Both toms thundered back. I felt I had a good chance to pull the 10-gauge's trigger and finish my quest to bag a bird with the "cannon," as well as solve the mystery of the beardless tom.

According to plan, the bird sailed down and eased into the grassy opening. When he saw the decoys, he dropped his wings and fanned his tail feathers. He stepped behind a big pine, and I adjusted my aim. When he stepped from behind the pine, I clucked loudly to pull him out of strut and lit the fire. At 32 steps, the 3-ounce load from the 10 gauge put the tom down for the count.

Rolling the gobbler on his back, I solved the beardless mystery. The tom sported not one, but two scraggly beards less than three inches long. The bird's breast feathers hid the beards from my view. Not surprising, the bird weighed 14½ pounds, but sported 1½-inch, needle-sharp, hooked spurs.

I must agree I have never fired any turkey gun and load combination that has put so many pellet holes in a turkey target. But after a week of lug-

ging the 12-pound artillery piece through the woods, I'm still not convinced that I have to shoot a 10-gauge to be a successful turkey hunter.

To be perfectly clear, I'm not anti-10-gauge, and I'm more than happy for any turkey hunter out there to shoot any legal-gauge they feel comfortable toting.

I'll share a little anecdote as to why I'm sticking with a 12-gauge. I was hunting during Iowa's fourth spring season with three longtime friends: well-known writer Jim Casada, Realtree's Dodd Clifton and Bug Tamer's public relations manager, Keane Maddey. I was shooting a Winchester Super X2 chambered for 3½-inch loads. I found a Trulock choke the gun liked and matched it with Winchester ammo's 3½-inch, high-velocity No. 4 loads. This gun puts 98 percent of its pattern in a 30-inch circle at 40 yards and keeps between 125 and 130 pellets in a 10-inch circle at that distance.

Casada was set up beside me at the edge of a cut cornfield where we had four longbeards strutting their stuff. I offered to let him shoot first, since he had never tagged an Iowa bird. After about 45 minutes, I called one of the birds into range and my friend shot. Bad luck and an errant vine caused his shot to cripple the gobbler. When Jim stood to finish the bird, he realized his leg had gone to sleep and fell flat on his face. He urged me

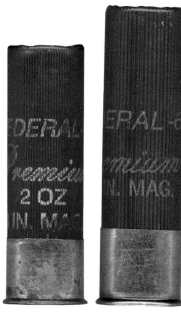

A 12-GAUGE 3-inch magnum (left) provides a powerhouse load, but is dwarfed by the 3½-inch 10 gauge.

to seal the deal.

I don't advocate shooting turkeys past 40 yards unless the bird is wounded, at which point all bets are off.

Conscientious turkey hunters should do everything in their power to finish what they started. I got a bead on that bird on the long side of 65 yards. When I pulled the trigger he went down like he'd been hit with a sack of hammers.

Again, for the sake of clarity, I am not advocating shooting turkeys beyond 40 yards. The point I want to make is this: If I've got a 12-gauge loaded with 3- or 3½-inch ammo and it will do the deed if I do my part, do I need to carry anything else?

9. Small-Bore Turkey Guns:
A Look at 20-gauge Shotguns for Turkey Hunting

"Waiting until a gobbler steps to within 25 or 30 yards before pulling the trigger just turns up the heat on an already high-tension game of wits."

THIS TEXAS Rio Grande was bagged with a Remington 1100 20-gauge.

The 3-inch magnum 12-gauge shotgun is undeniably the most popular choice of turkey hunters today, but the 20-gauge continues to pick up fans as the sport grows.

It's become doctrine that hunters should call toms to within 40 yards for quick, clean kills with today's heavy loads in 12-gauge guns. Some experienced hunters have upped the challenge of the sport by setting self-imposed range limits, relying on their calling ability to bring birds closer. Waiting until a gobbler steps to within 25 or 30 yards before pulling the trigger just turns up the heat on an already high-tension game of wits.

I had just such a match planned for a Texas Rio Grande hunt that had its beginnings at an earlier NWTF national convention. For the third straight year, Gary West, former NWTF director of marketing, asked me to guide a Texas turkey hunt to be auctioned at the Grand National Hunt Auction. When the auctioneer's gavel came down on Oregon chapter leader Jan Messersmith's high bid, the course was set for a challenging hunt on Whindam Ranch with outfitter Dave Gottschall from Clyde, Texas.

Over the next few weeks, I put a few 20-gauge shotguns to the test. Stepping up the challenge was former Remington press relations manager Bill Wohl. Bill suggested a Model 1100 semi-auto and Model 870 pump, both chambered for 3-inch shells. The lustrous, downsized semi-auto featured a 28-inch barrel, while the pump gun sported a dull matte finish and a 20-inch barrel. Both guns were threaded

for screw-in choke tubes, a necessity for getting the tightest patterns from modern 20-gauge magnum loads.

After a few trips to the range, the Model 1100, fitted with a Hastings extra-full choke tube, got the nod for the Texas trip. Preparations were complete once the gun's shiny exterior got a total camouflage tape job. Finding only a single uncooperative gobbler the first day, Jan suggested that we split up for the second morning's hunt, to double our chances of locating gobbling turkeys. (Who's to argue with a guy with more than 70 gobblers to his credit?)

Before dawn broke on day two, we headed for opposite ends of the ranch. As luck would have it, I found birds roosted in an oak grove mere feet across a fence on a neighboring ranch. Daylight came slowly as the wind howled and the sky opened up, dumping buckets of cold rainwater down my collar. When the lightning began, I felt allergic to holding a big chunk of steel in my hands. I quickly laid the Remington down, crawled several feet away and hunkered under a thorn bush. Every time the thunder would crack, a pair of longbeards let me know that they were in no hurry to turn lose of their roost limb.

The thunderhead passed 30 minutes later, and I got back into position under a mesquite tree and tried to call the toms through the fence and up to my soggy decoys. The dozen or so hens in the flock changed my perfect plan and led them deeper into the ranch, where I couldn't go. Options being what they were, I kept my sodden fanny parked under that mesquite.

A few minutes before 9 a.m., a tom tuned up across the fence, so I yelped back a lascivious lie. After several choruses of "Come On Over to My Place" were exchanged, the tom decided that now was better than later. He strutted up to the fence and spied Henrietta and Rocky, my hen and jake decoys, a few feet past my hideout. The bird slid under the fence and stretched to his full height. His posture was a mixture of pure lust and rage at seeing Rocky courting his girlfriend. He leaned into the wind and ran the 80 yards in nothing flat, flashed a half strut and commenced flogging my red-

headed decoy. A hard right cross from the longbeard's wing butt lifted the Feather Flex jake from its stake and into the air. A gust of wind caught the decoy and carried it several feet, the tom in hot pursuit. When the gobbler caught Rocky again, he spurred the decoy and stomped it into the mud. Rocky usually gets thumped in the early rounds, but he finishes strong. His rival never saw the knockout punch coming. At 10 yards, 1¼ ounces of Federal No. 6 shot has a way of changing the odds.

Later that afternoon, Jan and I returned to the scene of the earlier battle and had another gobbler announce his presence while I was reliving the victory. Rocky and Henrietta took their same positions, and Jan and I occupied the same mesquite tree. In less than four minutes, an overly inquisitive hen led her strutting suitor to 12 yards, and Jan's Beretta ended the contest just before Rocky got another drubbing.

Besides its abilities as a turkey taker at reduced ranges for experienced hunters willing to abide by self-imposed limitations, the 20-

31

gauge's lighter weight is a pleasure to carry in the field. And at the other end of the spectrum, the 20's lighter recoil is a time-tested winner for ladies and youth.

In the wake of the National Wild Turkey Federation's JAKES program, tens of thousands of New England Firearms' 20-gauge youth models have been put in the hands of many budding turkey hunters.

Dick Rosenlieb, vice president of NWTF Chapter and Membership Development, wanted to introduce his family to the sport. I suggested we outfit his wife, Linda, and their 10-year-old daughter, Lindsey, with the Remington 870 and NEF 20-gauge youth gun, respectively.

On Linda's first morning out for a wild turkey, Dick called a longbeard off the roost and into their laps. Linda obliged by clobbering the mature tom with one shot from the 20-gauge

pump gun. A few mornings later, Lindsey had a more difficult time choosing which one of seven jakes would go home with her. After all was said and done, the reduced weight of gun and recoil had the desired effect on their first turkey hunting experience–they couldn't wait for the next season.

No matter what the application–youth, lady or veteran hunter–matching extra-tight choke tubes with the best patterning load is the way to get the best performance from a 20 -gauge. After extensive testing, a 3-inch, 1¼-ounce load of No. 6 shot beat the same weight of No. 4s hands down. I like the No. 6s over the larger shot because they performed much more consistently. All the loads I tested with No. 4s produced ragged patterns with big gaps. With the guns and choke tubes tested, I would feel confident out to 30 yards with No. 6 shot, but not past 15 yards with the larger shot size. Your 20-gauge might shoot the larger shot better than what I experienced, so give it a thorough testing before making a final decision.

The chart below shows selected average loads using two Colonial Arms tubes and one Hastings extra-full choke tube shooting Remington and Federal 3-inch, 1¼-ounce loads of No. 6 shot

H20-GAUGE CHOKE AND AMMO COMPARISON

Gun	Choke Tube	Ammo	Pellets 30"	Percent	Head & Neck Circle
Rem. 1100	Colonial TK1	Rem.	174	62	5
Rem. 1100	Colonial TK2	Rem.	205	73	9
Rem. 1100	Hastings XF	Rem.	187	67	6
Rem. 1100	Colonial TK2	Fed.	230	82	12
Rem. 1100	Colonial TK 1	Fed.	224	80	13
Rem. 1100	Hastings XF	Fed.	237	84	20
Rem. 1100	Rem. IMP	Fed.	201	71	9*

* Remington improved cylinder used for comparison.

REMINGTON M 870 EXPRESS 20-GAUGE

ITHACA CLASSIC 37

NEF 20-GAUGE YOUTH

from a Remington Model 1100, 28-inch barrel. Testing was done on Winchester turkey patterning targets at 40 yards for comparison only.

My earliest memories of hunting with my father revolve around a single-shot 16-gauge that was passed down from his father. I remember tromping through woods and thickets with the well-worn "Long Tom," as my Grandpa Ernie nicknamed the full-choked meat-getter.

That relic, a product of the Bridge Gun Company, manufactured in the legendary Connecticut Valley during the first half of the 20th century, served a dual role. My grandpa kept it and other guns around his farmhouse to ward off intruders. Like most other country folks, a single-barrel shotgun also served to put

THE AUTHOR'S grandfather used this worn 16-gauge to put meat on the table during the Great Depression.

meat on the table during the Great Depression.

The old gun had seen a hard life. Its 30-inch full-choked barrel has a slight bulge near the muzzle. One of my dad's friends slipped and stuck the gun in the snow only to have a swamp rabbit jump from underfoot moments later. It's amazing that the gun didn't blow up in his hands. The catch holding the forearm to the barrel was worn to the point where several wraps of electrical tape were necessary

to keep the gun together. A slip-on recoil pad had been added at some point to tame its punchy kick.

The old 16-gauge was also the victim of a 13-year-old's first gunsmithing efforts. The gun was dressed up with a stock refinish and cold blue job, compliments of Birchwood Casey. When I found the gun in my Dad's closet a few years ago, hefting the old single-shot brought back a flood of memories. Long Tom accounted for my first rabbit,

squirrel and quail, and had accompanied my dad and me on our first deer hunt. Wild turkeys were long gone in the Missouri Bootheel and Southern Illinois when my dad was growing up, nor were they present in southeastern North Carolina when I was a boy. Long Tom was past due for a crack at a turkey.

To open the 1997 spring turkey season, I joined NWTF volunteer Richard Wansley to hunt his farm in north Georgia. After a couple of close encounters that morning, Richard suggested that we try his parents' farm nearby.

That afternoon, Richard, his youngest son, Jordan, and I shuffled into the woods, where the action picked up fast. We barely got inside the wood line when I heard a muffled half gobble. I dismissed the sound as my imagination, but a few seconds later we all heard gobbler yelps, which froze us in our tracks. Moments later three gobblers stepped into view about 90 yards away. Pinned down, we simply eased into a sitting position and got ready.

A few quiet yelps and the three jakes started moving in our direction. They got hung up on an old wire fence for several minutes, but one of the birds finally figured how to get through the hog wire. I was waiting for the bird to step from behind some briars when Richard hissed, "Shoot him." When the young tom walked to within 15 yards, Jordan obliged and put the bird in a pile with his 20-gauge Remington 870. The boy jumped up, but Richard grabbed him by the belt and pulled him to the ground. We kept calling while the other birds walked up to the fence and yelped several times. Over the course of the next hour, we watched a fascinating show. The remaining jakes gobbled and yelped in frustration, but couldn't quite figure out how to get over or through the fence. The standoff remained until the birds walked off to roost.

The next morning, Richard and I eased into the woods and set up on the other side of the fence, to eliminate the obstacle from our setup. Our plan worked fine until the gobblers sailed down within feet of where we had hunted them the day before—on the wrong side of the fence again. Turning around, I eased within 10 feet of the fence before Richard and I began calling.

Four jakes ran toward our setup. I waited for one of the birds to step away from the others and drew a bead. Even though part of the pattern hit the rotten fence, the bird went down for keeps. At 16 yards, my grandpa's single-shot 16-gauge was more than adequate for the job at hand.

Prior to the hunt, I tested the few available 16-gauge loads that would work in turkey hunting situations. The load that patterned the best was the Winchester Super X 1⅛ ounce of No. 6 shot. Just like the guns chambered for 16-gauge, loads are limited in comparison to today's 10-, 12- or 20-gauge loads. Looking back several years, the 16-gauge fell out of favor when the 3-inch 20-gauge was created. Equaling the 16-gauge in performance, the smaller 20-gauge magnum loads quickly eclipsed the once-popular 16-gauge. Even though the 16 has fallen from favor with gun-makers, several vintage guns still offer the turkey hunter another choice when pursuing these noble birds.

A couple of years ago, Ithaca began once again chambering their Model 37 pump guns in 16-gauge. These guns are special-order affairs, which has limited their numbers. Out of curiosity, and a bit of nostalgia, I asked Robin Sharpless, Ithaca's new publicity man, if it would be possible to create a 16-gauge turkey gun. We discussed how to set up the gun, and whether to fit it with a fancy camo job. Wanting to keep a more traditional look, I opted for a nonreflective matte blue finish for the metal and a hand-rubbed stock. True to his word, Robin had the craftsmen at Ithaca bob the barrel to 22 inches, mount rifle sights and thread it for a screw-in Colonial Arms choke. Although it wasn't necessary, the lightweight 16-gauge also got a barrel porting job.

As luck would have it, I hunted with the Ithaca several times during the 2001 spring season, but never got a chance to pull the trigger. The one-of-a-kind turkey gun would have done well enough, if given the chance. I patterned it with two custom Nitro loads, which did well for shots 25 yards and closer. These loads consisted of 1⅛ ounces of No. 5 or No. 6 shot. I also shot several test patterns with the same Winchester Super X loads that killed the Georgia jake four seasons before. These performed well enough to stretch the maximum range to 30 yards.

New 16-gauge shotguns are few and far between these days. In addition to the Ithaca Model 37, Stoeger offers a 16-gauge side-by-side double gun. I have not yet tried one of the Stoeger double-barrels on a patterning target, but I will soon. Remington also has ventured back into the 16-gauge arena with a new version of their Model 870 pump.

Considering that numerous 16-gauge guns have been relegated to the closet rather than used for turkey hunting, I wonder if a new turkey load would create a revival for fans of the 16-gauge. Given the limitations of the 2¾-inch shells and a maximum payload of 1⅛ ounces, a denser pattern could possibly be achieved by going to a smaller shot size. A few years ago Federal added a 2-ounce load of No. 7½ shot to their 3-inch 12-gauge magnum loads. The load found favor with a few turkey hunters, owing to the tremendous pellet count. More than 700 pellets could be squeezed into a 2-ounce load. The only downside of a load incorporating 7½ shot is that these smaller pellets shed velocity quicker than heavier 6s, 5s or 4s. After 30 yards, 7½ shot slows to the point where penetration pales in comparison to larger shot sizes. Inside of 30 yards, though, 7½ shot make deadly turkey medicine. Loading the 16-gauge with a charge of 7½ shot makes sense when striving for higher pellet counts.

SMALLER GAUGES can be deadly, but hunters should know their limitations.

III. A Choice of Hardware

If you compare sales figures, turkey hunters shoot semi-autos, pump actions and a handful of other action types. This section shares my hands-on experience with many of the popular models that are carried afield in spring and fall.

10. Semi-Auto Shotguns

The semi-autoloading shotgun has become the gun of choice for many of today's turkey hunters. Quick follow-up shots are one benefit provided by a semi-auto. As it relates to turkey hunting, second and subsequent shots are ready almost instantly without any further movements on the shooter's part.

After firing nearly 10,000 rounds of powerhouse turkey loads, I favor the semi-auto for another reason. By their design and function, semi-auto shotguns produce less recoil with the same loads than with other action types of equal gun weight. By design, auto-loading shotguns use some of the energy produced by firing a round to cycle the action. Gas-operated guns, such as the Beretta Extrema, bleed off a portion of the expanding propellant gas, which provides the most recoil reduction. The Benelli Super Black Eagle and other recoil-operated guns use the rearward inertia to cycle the action

QUICK FOLLOW-UP shots offered by a semi-auto can save a hunt.

and load another round. Either operating system helps soak up some of the force exerted on the shooter's shoulder and face.

My experience with guns featured in this and subsequent chapters in this section varies from brief patterning and evaluation sessions to extensive range testing and actual hunting use. I'll be the first to admit that I have owned several "pet" turkey guns that have been welcome companions in the turkey woods, as well as being top performers. The following guns are a representative cross section of popular turkey gun models. I have no doubt that a fair number of turkey hunters reading this book will not find their favorite turkey gun mentioned. That fact is not meant to be a slight against their gun of choice, but an honest indication that I have not had the pleasure of shooting or hunting the most noble of game birds with their version of turkey gun perfection.

My earliest experience with the Benelli line of shotguns was with the now-discontinued Black Eagle model owned by longtime friend Paul Cook. It was chambered for 12-gauge 3-inch magnum loads. I was quickly impressed with the gun's dependability while we hunted ducks in the swamps of West Tennessee. Grit, grime and the rigors imposed by hunting flooded timber didn't hamper the performance of this workhorse one bit. On other occasions I have patterned other Black Eagles, and found their performances acceptable.

The United States Marine Corps gave Benelli high marks in engineering when it selected the M4 military-pattern autoloader as the newest combat shotgun for the 21st century. Terrorist-hunting Marines have swept their share of Afghanistan caves with the Benelli M4, which speaks volumes about the performance capabilities of Benelli shotguns.

Benelli shotguns are manufactured in Urbino, Italy, and were imported by Heckler & Koch, Inc. prior to 1998. Then Benelli USA was purchased by Beretta Holdings Corporation and moved to Accokeek, Maryland.

Benelli's Black Eagle
Another Black Eagle I've had experience with

was the personal turkey gun owned by noted gunsmith Mark Bansner from Adamstown, Pennsylvania. I did a meager bit of informal pattern testing with this gun while on a hunt at Pete Clare's Turkey Trot Acres, in Candor, New York, in 1993. As expected, this gun threw tight patterns at 40 yards. Bansner has earned a good reputation for tuning up turkey guns to improve their performance. Several turkey hunters I know have sent their guns to Bansner for a tune-up, and speak his praise.

On average, Benelli shotgun barrels have tighter internal bore diameters than American-made 12-gauge guns. The tighter bores are due to the requirements of the Benelli's recoil-operated action's need for higher chamber pressure to function with lighter loads. Correspondingly, I have found that Benellis tend to pattern turkey loads best with tighter chokes. When I am patterning a Benelli, I will usually start with a tube that has a diameter of .655. Some of the bores that measure closer to .720 may perform better with an even tighter .650-sized tube. Since Benellis are recoil-operated, they will produce slightly more recoil than a gas-operated autoloader. The addition of a mercury recoil reducer is recommended for lengthy patterning sessions. Once hunting sea-

A 12-GAUGE Benelli M-1 is one of the author's favorites.

son rolls around, I remove the recoil reducer in favor of carrying a lighter-weight gun. One thing's for certain, the Benelli Inertia Recoil System generates a little more recoil, but the little extra push is compensated for by speed. A Benelli is the fastest cycling semi-auto, bar none.

Benelli M1 Field

Benelli's M1 Field shotguns are no-nonsense tools that combine firepower and ruggedness in a package that's all business. The proven Benelli inertia system can handle whatever you put in the magazine, from soft-kicking $1^{1}/_{8}$-ounce target ammo to the stiffest turkey loads or rifled slugs. It's fast-feeding and, above all, reliable in every weather condition.

Sportsmen want durable, long-wearing, low-visibility finishes that won't spook game but will stand up to tough hunting conditions. The M1 Field is available with matte-finish metal combined with black synthetic stocks or more traditional satin-finished wal-

nut. For the ultimate in concealment, it has been offered in Realtree X-Tra Brown camouflage, or more recently in Advantage Timber High Definition camouflage. Barrels are available in 21-, 24-, 26- or 28-inch lengths, all with ventilated ribs. Cylinder, improved cylinder, modified, improved modified and full choke tubes are supplied. Even the southpaw is covered with a left-hand version. When you need the right tool for the job, nothing beats the versatility of the M1 Field. If I had to own only one shotgun for turkey hunting, it would be an M1 Field with a 24-inch barrel.

Benelli Super Black Eagle

In the early 1990s, Benelli introduced the world's first autoloader designed to tame the recoil of the potent 12 gauge 3½-inch shell: the Super Black Eagle. The Benelli inertia system enables this auto to handle a full range of ammunition from 2½-inch, 3 dram, 1⅛-oz. target loads to the thumping 3½-inch magnum

goose loads without a hiccup.

The Super Black Eagle's modest weight and superb balance make it a truly universal auto for all types of shooting and hunting.

A left-hand version is offered in matte synthetic or Realtree Advantage Timber High Definition camouflage with a 24-, 26- or 28-inch barrel. Flinching as empty shells pass through the shooter's sightline or struggling with controls on the wrong side of the gun are no longer problems for the left-handed shooter.

Since its introduction, the Super Black Eagle has become the standard by which other 3½-inch 12-gauge autoloaders are judged. Its success has paved the way for a variety of imitators, but it remains unsurpassed in reliability, shootability and durability. If I could only own one shotgun for all hunting applications, it would be a Super Black Eagle fitted with a 26-inch barrel.

New for 2003, Benelli will offer pistol-grip-stocked Super Black Eagles and M1 Field models. These guns will be dressed in Advantage Timber High Definition camo. I have modified several of my turkey guns, as well as working with manufacturers, such as Mossberg, to design functional pistol-grip turkey guns. Benelli's decision to offer this configuration is a first for any of the major gunmakers selling specialty turkey guns. The ergonomics of a pistol grip makes it easier to control the

Benelli's Inertia Recoil—How It Works

Cycle of Operation

Feeding—When the cartridge drop lever is pressed, the rear portion of the carrier latch is released, causing the front of the latch to pivot away from the centerline, which releases a shell from the magazine tube onto the carrier. As the shell is thrown to the rear by the force of the magazine spring, it presses the carrier latch back into position where it is engaged by the drop lever. (This prevents multiple shells from being thrown out of the magazine.) As the bolt moves forward under pressure from the expanding recoil spring, the bolt head contacts the top of the shell rim and begins moving the shell forward. At the same time, the carrier lifts the front of the shell, positioning it to be fed into the chamber.

Chambering—As the bolt pushes the shell forward, the carrier guides it into the chamber until the shell rim comes to rest in the counterbore at the chamber opening. As the round seats into the chamber, the extractor (located on the bolt head) contacts the ramped relief cut in the right side of the barrel. This forces the extractor away from the shell and allows it to completely seat in the chamber. The locking head is now momentarily at rest against the back of the shell.

Locking—The bolt group, being pushed by the recoil spring, applies pressure to the base of the shell. As the bolt body moves forward, the locking head pin cams along a track, causing the locking head to rotate counterclockwise. This rotation engages the locking lugs with the locking recesses in the barrel extension, thereby locking the bolt head to the barrel. The extractor remains away from the shell.

Firing—The trigger is pulled, which releases the sear, which in turn releases the hammer. The hammer strikes the firing pin and overcomes the tension of the firing pin spring, driving the pin into the primer. The primer detonates, igniting the propellant powder to fire the shell.

Unlocking—The recoil impulse of the fired shell creates an impact on the locking head, which passes recoil energy to all connected components—including the shooter. The locking head is connected to the barrel, which is connected in turn to the receiver, trigger group, and buttstock. All of these components—plus the shooter—begin a rearward recoil motion. The only part that remains motionless is the bolt body, which is suspended between the recoil spring in the rear and the inertia spring in front. Recoil energy causes all components to travel rearward except for the bolt body. This action causes the inertia spring to be compressed. The spring is very strong and the compression only lasts a few milliseconds. The spring then expands, imparting its stored energy into the bolt body, finally causing the body to begin moving rearward. As the bolt body moves rearward, the locking head pin travels in its track and causes the bolt head to rotate clockwise. This action unlocks the bolt lugs from the barrel extension recesses, thus unlocking the bolt.

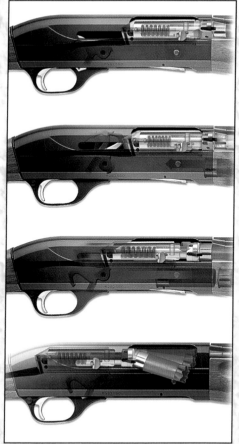

WINCHESTER'S Super X2 NWTF Trade Gun cycles both 3- and 3½-inch 12- gauge ammo.

chester's new semi-auto Super X2 12 gauge.

About 10 a.m., we drove out to get a bite of breakfast. As an afterthought, Mark decided to create a salt lick in one of his whitetail honey holes, across the road from where we had been hunting. Mark had a spade in his hands, and I was hefting a 50-pound sack of livestock salt when a gust of wind from the northwest carried a distant gobble to our ears. When we heard the second faint gobble, we traded shovel for shotgun and went to investigate. As we closed the distance, we got the birds to occasionally answer a crow call. Closing the gap to 100 yards, we found a pair of soggy longbeards and three hens in a pasture. The hens were already heading our way, so we sat tight and waited for the gobblers to follow.

The toms must have known that the hens were more interested in nesting, because they didn't bother to tag along. We began calling when the hens were past, but the gobblers already had made up their minds to head the other way, looking for better company. A deep ditch lay along the fence where the birds were strutting and gobbling, so we used the cover to close the distance and get adjacent to the traveling toms. Cecil and I eased into position. Mark was between us with his video camera. Some loud yelps and cutting turned the birds around, with the subordinate gobbler anxiously poking his head through the fence to get a look at the hen he heard in the ditch below. The boss bird gobbled several times and started moving back down the fence toward our setup. Just as he got into range, he started moving up the hill, away from the fence. Aiming between the strands, I lined up the sights on the Winchester Super X2 and lit the fire. The 1¾-ounce High Energy load of Federal No. 6 shot found its mark, and the bird went down for keeps. Lady Luck wasn't through with us yet. During the hourlong hunt, it was apparent that the bird had a good beard and was a heavyweight champ. When I went to retrieve him I found that he carried a matching set of 1½-inch spurs to complement his 24-pound bulk and 10-inch beard.

Back in camp we reviewed video footage and

gun and hold it steady for long periods of time in comfort.

Winchester Super X2

Rain can make spring turkey hunting miserable, but wind can make it nearly impossible. When both forces of nature clasp hands, just hearing a gobbling bird is a matter of luck. And that's just how it played out on an early May hunt in Iowa in the spring of 1999.

Braving a light rain and 30-mile-per-hour gusts, M.A.D. Calls' Mark Drury, Cecil Carder of Bass Pro Shops and I tried to get something going from the roost, but the turkeys had different ideas. My primary mission on the hunt was to gather some field experience with Win-got a dramatic replay of the hunt, and in particular, the performance of the Comp-N-Choke .675 tube and Super X2 doing its intended job. The combination, matched with the Federal High Energy ammo, put a devastating swarm of shot along the bird's neck and head at 40 yards.

A hurried patterning session prior to the Iowa hunt produced some eye-opening results with the Super X2 and Comp-N-Choke tubes. It was my original intention to mate some of today's high-velocity turkey loads with the gun to find a tight shooting combination. The gun is chambered for 3½-inch magnum 12-gauge shells, and will interchangeably fire 3-inch magnums or 2¾-inch field loads. It performed flawlessly with the 2¾-inch Winchester AA dove loads and 3-inch magnum turkey loads. The exception was the powerful 3½-inch magnum high velocity Winchester turkey loads. The 3½-inch hulls were deformed, and failed to eject. I was a little disappointed, since I had envisioned finding a choke and gun combination that would pattern well with Winchester's high-velocity 2-oz. load of No. 4 shot in the 3½-inch chambering. When I backed off and went to the 3-inch turkey loads, I experienced no problems with ejection. I returned the gun to Winchester and learned that the ejector pin was placed in the wrong position at the factory. A quick

adjustment and the gun was returned in three days. From that point on, I had no problems ejecting the 3½-inch shells.

Two loads gave excellent results: Federal's high-energy load of No. 6s in tandem with the Comp-N-Choke .675 tube; and Winchester-Olin's high-velocity loads of No. 5 shot through a CNC .670 tube. The Super X2 semi-auto has a back-bored barrel which has been bored beyond the forcing cone to a slightly greater width than the standard bore diameter, which measures nearly 10 gauge in size. These tubes are also interchangeable with Browning Invector Plus chokes.

At 7 pounds, 3 ounces, the Super X2 carries well in the field. Black synthetic stocks and a black matte finish make this an all-weather gun, and it functioned well in the rainy conditions I experienced.

Browning Gold

The Browning Gold line of semi-autos is manufactured in Japan. I have patterned several of these guns in preparation for their use on the NWTF's *Turkey Call* television show. I've fired both 12- and 20-gauge guns, and find their performances and functions very similar to the Winchester Super X2. The previous data for the Super X2 is a good indicator of what a 12-

WINCHESTER SUPER X-2
NWTF TURKEY 3½ INCH

BROWNING GOLD 12-GAUGE

REMINGTON 11-87
SPS-T 3½ INCH

HUNTING AS PART of a team in Alabama, a turkey hunter draws a bead with a Remington 11-87 12-gauge.

gauge Gold will prefer in chokes and loads.

Remington's Semi-Autos

The Model 11-87 SPS-T Mossy Oak camo version brings gas-operated recoil reduction to the heavy magnum world of today's turkey hunters. For dense, turkey-taking patterns, the Rem Choke system on this shotgun is supplied with a Turkey Super Full Rem Choke tube. The short, 21-inch vent rib barrel comes with a white front and steel mid-bead. A synthetic stock resists both the elements and hard use. Note: 21-inch Model 11-87 turkey and deer barrels are not pressure-compensated and are not for use with target or light field loads. The length of pull is 14 inches, with a 1½-inch drop at comb and a 2½-inch drop at heel.

The Model 11-87 SPS-T Camo RS/TG comes equipped with rifle sights, which make it easier to adjust the point of aim to a particular load's point of impact. If you wish to add a scope to a new Remington turkey gun, you may wish to opt for the 11-87 SPS-T Camo CL model, which comes equipped with a cantilever scope mount.

I have vast experience with an older 11-87 version. It is an NWTF trade version that was sold in 1992. It is covered in a reduced-pattern of Trebark camo. I have killed scores of gobblers with this gun and find it to be one of my favorites. It performs well with the factory Extra Full turkey choke and a variety of other tubes that measure in the .665 range. This gun has a preference for Winchester Hi-Velocity No. 5s, as well as the new HEVI•SHOT turkey loads. The tungsten-nickel HEVI•SHOT loads perform better from a .675 or larger choke.

Wind may be the ultimate nemesis for spring turkey hunters. Straight to the point, the harder it blows, the less you can hear, and accurate shooting is handicapped.

Stepping from the plane at the San Antonio airport in April 2001, my first emotion was optimism tinged with a little doubt as the wind kicked up dust on the tarmac. I was there with Remington's Linda Powell and Eddie Stevenson, along with writers Dave Henderson and Bob McNally, to put Big Green's newest turkey gun to the test.

During the two-hour ride to Medart, Texas,

Linda and Eddie brought us up to speed on the refinements of the just-released Model 11-87 semi-auto chambered in 3½-inch magnum. Adding to the super-magnum chambering was a new turkey choke design and hot new turkey loads.

By the time we pulled off the narrow blacktop onto a dusty ranch road, the wind had picked up a notch to 25-mph gusts. As I stepped out of the van to open the metal ranch gate, I shook my head and hoped that the wind would die down by morning.

Anxious to get started, we stowed our gear and headed to the range, which was conveniently located out the back door of Keyhole Outfitters' ranch house.

A two-hour session at the shooting bench proved productive as each of us took turns sighting and patterning the heavy-hitting 3½-inch 11-87s and 3½-inch chambered Model 870 pump guns. Some of the guns were fitted with scopes; others sported adjustable rifle sights. I quickly came to appreciate the gun's raised comb, which served the purpose of perfectly aligning the shooter's eye with either open sights or scopes.

Coupling the turkey-hunter-friendly stock dimensions with a new Remington choke tube and high-velocity loads produced good patterns at turkey hunting ranges. All the while, the strong headwind continued to increase. With each shot, the white shot buffer was blown back in my face, which emphasized the need for proper eye protection during any shooting session.

After a quick breakfast the next morning, Bob McNally joined our guide and me for a quick ride to a nearby pasture that was reported to be loaded with willing gobblers.

Standing on the dark Texas two-track, Bob and I whispered about the difference in definitions of "pasture." When in Texas, a pasture takes on a more generalized meaning. Where I'm from in the South, pasture refers to an open, grassy place where cows graze. Not so in Texas. This pasture was like many of the other Lone Star State pastures I'd seen plenty of grazing, but a landscape filled with cactus, mesquite, live oaks and a host of other things that will stab or poke things best left ungouged.

When the Rio Grande tom gobbled the second time, I thought I had him sufficiently coursed. With the wind still coming in gusts, it was pretty reasonable that he was roosted upwind of our listening spot. Looping around several live oak thickets, we closed the gap to within 150 yards of the loudmouthed bird. Easing through the last cover, I sat against a skinny live oak, facing the gobbler, while Bob covered the back door. On the way to our setup we had heard other turkeys gobbling, so it

WINCHESTER SUPER X2 12 GAUGE

Manufacturer	Shot Size	Weight	Choke	10"	No. in Vitals	% in 10"
Federal	6	1¾	CNC .670	75	17	19
Federal	6	1¾	CNC .675	128	32	33
Federal	6	1¾	CNC .680	82	19	21
Federal	4	1¾	CNC .670	74	29	35
Federal	4	1¾	CNC .675	68	17	29
Federal	4	1¾	CNC .680	58	16	25
Winchester	4	1¾	CNC .680	58	16	25
Winchester	5	1¾	CNC .670	102	28	34
Winchester	5	1¾	CNC .675	91	24	31
Winchester	5	1¾	CNC .680	84	35	28

other. About that time a fine Rio gobbler followed on their back trail. At the sight of the hens he gobbled and went into full strut, the wind almost bowling him over in the process. It was going to be a challenge, but Bob managed to move his gun into position and draw a bead on the gobbler's head. The Remington roared and the hens took flight, heading toward Mexico. The 25-yard distance was a chip shot for the 11-87 stuffed with a powerhouse 3½-inch load of No. 4 shot.

One bird hung up to prevent it from becoming coyote food, we headed off to find another bird for me. An hour later we were in contact with another longbeard. We set up and called, but could not get the bird to budge from his strut zone. We moved up twice more, the last time close enough to convince the tom to come looking for us. Long story short, I set up with two obvious opposing choices for the bird's approach—and picked the wrong one. I could hear the gobbler drumming, but couldn't tell from which side of the thicket he would approach. He was so close when he gobbled that it didn't help me decide which direction he would come from. When he rounded a bush at five yards while I aimed 45 degrees to his right, the outcome was academic—one scared turkey and one frustrated hunter.

Over the next couple of days the wind blew and the hunting

was wise to cover as many angles as possible.

As in many turkey hunting adventures, things seldom turn out like they're planned. The bird we were set up on had other things on his mind. He gobbled to everything we threw at him, but to no avail. We watched as he crossed the pasture no closer than 130 yards as he headed to another part of the ranch. Without

warning, a hen trotted around a clump of brush that was behind me and in front of Bob. Within seconds a second hen raced to catch up with the first hen. They stood in front of us searching for that lonesome hen that had been raising such a fuss. At five yards, the lead hen glared at my camouflaged form with one eye, snapping her head around to bore a hole in me with the

got tougher. Bob and I continued hunting together and even switched locations by several miles on our guide's advice. We wound up prospecting on a new property that Keyhole had leased that spring. Either we would get into turkeys or we wouldn't. I liked the prospect of hunting birds that hadn't been harried by hunters, so it was a go.

We drove a mile deep into the pasture, then hiked a mile farther, calling frequently to try and raise a gobble. After an hour and several attempts, I got a response when I hammered a series of cutts on my trusty Rohm Brothers walnut box call. I hit the call a second time and the bird's faint gobble drifted back on the stiff breeze. We set up once again, and not one, but two longbeards came calling. I set up facing the direction of the gobbles, while Bob set up to cover my left side and rear. As luck would have it, the pair of toms skirted our setup wide to the left, giving Bob the only shot. He picked a 3-foot gap in the brush, waited for one of the gobblers to step into the clear, took careful aim and lit the fire.

After a short chase, we retrieved Bob's bird. After the dust settled, I walked back to the spot where the gobbler had been standing when shot, and surveyed the situation. I have learned a lot about shooting turkeys by carefully studying the bird's location and the path the shot traveled from the muzzle. I plucked my laser rangefinder from my vest and measured the distance to where Bob had been sitting. I got a reading of 46 yards, a pretty stiff poke for any turkey gun—especially one fresh out of the box. Reconstructing the shot, I saw what had caused Bob to underestimate his range. He had been sitting in shade, and his shooting lane was a dark tunnel through brush. When the gobbler stepped into the clear, the bird was standing in full sunlight. When that situation occurs, it's rather easy for an adrenaline-charged hunter to miss range estimation by a six- to 10-yard margin.

By the following afternoon, I was still itching to put a tag on a Rio gobbler. We went back to the same pasture from the day before to locate the running mate to Bob's earlier tom. Luck,

and a welcome lack of wind, was with us. We struck two different birds and moved in. One of the gobblers hung up on the wrong side of the fence, but the other tom continued to answer our calls from over 500 yards away. Using terrain and cover, we looped around the bird, trying to get as close as possible. The pasture looked like a park, with much of the understory bulldozed clean. Erring on the side of caution, we set up well back from where we thought the bird was located. When he answered us, a couple of times, I elected to get closer. We closed the gap another 100 yards or so, and set up again. Within five minutes we repeated our sneak, when it appeared that we could indeed get closer to the interested tom.

After the third setup, I waited about five minutes before calling. I gently stroked the box call, and the bird answered before I could finish the five-note yelp. He was close. I could see for 85 yards in the bird's direction, and he sounded not much farther. I decided to wait him out. When he gobbled the second time, I cut off his call with a series of cutts on a mouth call. Inside of 30 seconds, the gobbler walked into view at the far end of the clearing. I watched as the tom stopped to strut and gobble several times as he closed the last 50 yards. After working several days to get a crack at a gobbler, I decided to be patient and enjoy the show as long as possible. When the gobbler passed 25 yards, I clucked once to bring his head up, and squeezed the trigger. Remington's 11-87 Super Mag shines under field conditions.

Beretta's turkey guns

Afternoon turkey hunting in Iowa can be red hot, so I was anxious to get in the woods from the moment the jet's tires barked on the Omaha runway. As soon as we gathered some stragglers in our crew of outdoor writers and representatives from Beretta, Winchester-Olin ammo and Hunter's Specialties, we were ready to make the hour's drive into the Loess Hills near Soldier, Iowa. I had been anticipating this return trip to Iowa to tag-team turkeys with Roger Hook once again.

One of the focal points of this trip would be

**REMINGTON MODEL 11-87
SPS-T SUPER MAGNUM**

running a Beretta AL 390 12-gauge through its paces with Winchester's high-velocity 1¾-ounce loads. I was hesitant about hunting the big birds without testing the Beretta at the range before the trip. I was, however, familiar with Winchester's new turkey load, and had put several other shotguns through testing with positive results. I decided to hedge my bet, and included in my gear a Kick's Gobblin' Thunder choke tube to fit the Beretta.

Quickly getting dressed in camo, several writers moseyed to outfitter Judd Cooney's shooting range behind the camp house. Nothing sophisticated for this crowd. A turkey target taped to the side of a cardboard box 40 yards out in the back pasture would tell us everything we wanted to know about the Beretta 390's performance–that it could "deliver the mail" consistently at 40 yards. One thing I noticed was that the gun I was shooting, which was fitted with the Gobblin' Thunder tube, was outperforming the guns with the factory tubes by a noticeable margin.

Roger Hook and I got to the woods at 4 p.m. and a huge gobbler with a thick beard was standing in the cornfield when we drove up. We backed out of sight and rolled out of the truck. Roger and I sneaked back and glassed to find the

bird again in order to map out a game plan. We circled out of sight and climbed the hill behind the bird. Another tom gobbled from a ridge 100 yards ahead of us, so we modified our plan and set up by a double-trunked oak tree to work the bird. Roger called while we trained our guns on an open flat ahead of us, in hopes that the bird would come straight to the call. Roger did an excellent job working this bird. When the bird seemed to cool off after Roger cutt hard, he backed off on the aggressive calling and the bird continued his slow advance.

After 30 minutes, the bird moved within 40 yards and began to strut and drum in the thicket below. Roger spied the bird moving from right to left toward another opening. Continuing to circle to our left, the bird dropped into a ditch and gave me a chance to move. Bracing the gun against the trunk, I waited for the tom to step into the clearing.

I saw him for the first time in a half-strut at 40 yards, but couldn't get a shot because of obstructions. Several tense moments passed as Roger whispered his pleas for me to shoot and the bird gobbled a half-dozen times. I held fire until the gobbler was in the clear, then took careful aim.

A few scant pounds of finger pressure dropped the sear,

slamming the Beretta AL390's firing pin into the Winchester primer, igniting the 1¾-ounce high-velocity load of Winchester No. 5s. Leaving the 24-inch barrel at about 1,250 fps –hot by today's turkey-load standards–the swarm of copper-plated shot found its intended mark and brought the exciting hunt to a fitting conclusion.

Back at camp, Roger and I learned that we were the only team to score that evening. When I later dressed the bird, I found 14 pellet strikes in the head and neck, which was plenty to put the 22½-pound bird down for the count.

Since I had tagged out, my gun went back in the rack for the remainder of the trip, but the choke tube was passed among the other writers in camp. Maybe I could've taken bids on the tube after its stellar performance on paper and in the woods.

Beretta shotguns have long been top performers in competition circles. Their rugged constitutions make them a top choice for shooters who fire thousands of rounds each year. Transfer this strength to shotguns made for turkey hunting applications and it handles today's hot turkey loads with good results.

Combining Beretta's five centuries of excellent craftsmanship with the National

BERETTA AL 391 XTREMA

Wild Turkey Federation's leadership created an opportunity to bring four turkey guns to the attention of a large segment of America's turkey hunters.

The first version of the AL390 included in the NWTF promotion is a 12-gauge version dressed in Realtree X-Tra Brown camouflage with a matching sling. This gun is chambered for 3-inch magnum loads, has a 24-inch barrel and an extended screw-in turkey choke tube. TRUGLO fiber-optic sights will aid in keeping this tight-shooting turkey gun on target. Rounding out the custom features of this AL390 is an NWTF medallion inlaid in the grip cap.

The next version of the AL390 is a matte black synthetic version with the same custom add-ons as the previous model. An NWTF youth model AL390 in 20 gauge has a matte-finished receiver, barrel, and a walnut stock, which also includes an NWTF medallion in the grip cap. A Beretta ES100 NWTF Special model was offered in Mossy Oak Break Up camo. An extra-full turkey choke, and TRUGLO sights customized the 24-inch barrel.

The world's oldest gun company launched the Extrema, their first 3½-inch 12 gauge, in 2002. The action's rotating bolt head is similar in design to the Benelli semi-autos, but the Extrema adds the cycling assist of a gas-operated system. The barrel is over-bored, which should help get the most from heavy turkey loads.

Mossberg's Semi-Auto

O. F. Mossberg and Sons is best known as a leading maker of pump-action shotguns. However, the gunmaker offered the Model 9200 3-inch 12 gauge for several years until it was discontinued in 2000. I've had a 24-inch-barreled version in Mossy Oak camo that has proven to be a winner in the turkey woods. This gun was the first turkey gun I used to pattern Winchester's High-Velocity turkey loads, and the two proved to be a winning combo. Winchester's High-Velocity 1½-ounce load of No. 4 or 5 shot is tops for this gun. Prior to testing Winchester high velocity loads, this gun proved a champ with the same company's revamped 2-ounce turkey loads. I've also had good luck with Federal Premium High-Velocity loads.

This 9200 has been fitted with a Speed Feed pistol-grip stock and a Simmons red-dot scope. Loaded with fast loads, this combo has taken several gobblers at extended ranges. I typically don't recommend that shots be taken at ranges greater than 40 yards, but this gun presents an exception to the rule. It consistently puts a swarm of pellets on target at ranges past 50 yards. The retained energy from a No. 4 or No. 5 pellet put on target will consistently kill a gobbler at distances beyond 40 yards. A hunt in Texas yielded just one of the many gobblers this gun has hammered at ranges beyond 40 yards.

On the third morning of a Spring 2000 hunt for Rio Grande gobblers near Eutopia, Texas, I called up a longbeard for writer Ron Spomer. We worked another gobbler for a couple of hours so I could fill my second tag, but couldn't catch up with the traveling tom.

After we got back to the ranch house, I still had a hankering to tag a gobbler. I told outfitter Steve Packer that I wanted to walk from camp and try to locate a gobbler. Walking toward a plowed crop field where a bird was seen the evening before, I set up and started calling. A bird answered behind me from several hundred yards away, so I kept calling. I moved in on the gobbler and set up about 100 yards away. Peering through my binoculars, I spied a strutter, a few jakes and some hens. The tom kept answering, but finally went silent. I crawled up to investigate, and the birds were gone. I went to survey the area where he had been strutting and found a brushy

ditch. Frustrated, I cutt loudly on a mouth call, and the bird answered from the other side of the ditch. I dropped down and counted six jakes, a hen and a longbeard. I put the Simmons red-dot on the longbeard, but a screen of brush hid him. A jake saw me, spooked and trotted off. The longbeard stood frozen for at least a minute before finally stepping out. I lit the fire behind a Federal High-Velocity load of No. 5s, and the bird went into a pile. I came back an hour later with my laser rangefinder, and it read 54 yards to where the gobbler had stood. The bird's 10¹⁄₁₆-inch beard and 1½-inch spurs are a fitting trophy that will remind me of how well this gun performs in real hunting situations.

Stoeger Model 2000

This gun is a real sleeper. When Benelli acquired Stoeger Industries in 2001, they added a new product to the Stoeger shotgun line: the Model 2000. Offered with a traditional walnut or a black synthetic stock, this gun may become one of my new favorites. I'll admit that this gun is at the lower end of the price scale when stacked up against other semi-autos, but it has some features that put it in a class by itself. The heart of any turkey gun is the barrel,

and this gun has something special going for it. The barrel is made in a Beretta factory and shipped abroad for final assembly. The same attention-to-detail machining that goes into more expensive guns also goes into this gun.

In early 2002, Stoeger offered the Model 2000 in a combination package with a smoothbore slug barrel with adjustable rifle sights. It accepts the same chokes that will fit a Beretta or Benelli 12 gauge. Couple this craftsmanship with one of the finest trigger pulls to be found on a factory gun, and it promises to be a real thumper. My first patterning sessions with a Model 2000 looked promising, with the usual high-velocity turkey loads shooting well. The adjustable sights made it a snap to bring the point of impact to the point of aim, and they're much sturdier than any of the fiber optic sights I've used for the past few seasons.

NWTF 1995 Gun of the Year–Franchi 610 VSL by American Arms

The National Wild Turkey Federation's Gun of the Year for 1995 followed the tradition of beautiful craftsmanship coupled with reliable functioning tailored to suit the most discriminating turkey hunter.

Several shotguns were considered during the selection process, according to Gary West, then NWTF director of marketing, but the nod went to American Arms' custom-crafted Franchi (pronounced FRAHN-kee) 610 VSL 12-gauge semi-automatic. This NWTF Gun of the Year was sold through fund-raising banquets, which accounts for its limited exposure to turkey hunters. The 610 VSL is a lightweight, gas-operated semi-auto that boasted good looks and muscle, being equipped to handle heavy 3-inch magnum loads, or light 2¾-inch field loads interchangeably. The stocks are fancy grade European walnut protected by a durable urethane finish. A slim black rubber recoil pad blends with the gun's stylish looks. Length of pull measures 14⅛ inches.

The receiver displays a roll-engraved woodland scene by NWTF CEO Rob Keck. Three gold turkeys in flight are shown on the left side, while a gobbler struts for his hen on the action side. (Collectors will be interested in the fact that Feathermate game bird knives by Benchmark, decorated with matching artwork, were also offered at banquets.) The receiver is matte-finished and the barrel has a medium-luster blued finish. The trigger, safety button and bolt release are

49

gold-plated. Each gun is seri-alized, with a limited edition of 600.

The most striking difference in the Franchi and past NWTF guns-of-the-year is barrel length. The 1995 gun sported a 26-inch vent-rib barrel. This barrel length was a bit longer than previous NWTF guns, and a compromise for hunters wishing to take their guns afield for turkeys or upland game. The longer sighting radius swings on flying game more smoothly, while still functional in all but the tight-est situations. At 7 pounds, 2 ounces, the 610 VSL's light weight makes it ideal for hunters who also like to spend their autumn days following beagles or bird dogs.

The 610 VSL is fitted with Franchi's Franchoke system, which offers six sizes of inter-changeable choke tubes rang-ing from skeet to Extra full. The full choke measures .685 inch, while the Extra full tube mikes .680 inch. Improved cylinder, modified and full choke tubes came with each NWTF gun.

As with other shotguns, the prototype Franchi 610 NWTF gun had a marked preference for particular magnum turkey loads. Patterning tests were conducted with several brands, loads and shot sizes. All patterning was done with full-choke tubes. The best pat-terns came from Federal's 3-inch, 2-ounce loads of No. 5 shot, which averaged 76 per-cent within a 30-inch circle at 40 yards. A near equal per-former was Winchester's 2¾-inch, 1½-ounce load of No. 4s, which averaged 72 percent. Toward the other end of the spectrum were two Win-chester loads: 2 ounces of No. 5s, which averaged 62percent; and 2 ounces of No. 6s, which averaged 53percent at 40 yards. This example just rein-forces the good ethics of pat-terning a shotgun before hunting with it. Each gun is an individual, capable of pat-terning some loads much tighter than others.

Franchi 612 and 912

Franchi was purchased by Benelli USA in 2000. Two models in the Franchi line are the 3-inch 12-gauge Model 612 and the 3½-inch magnum Model 912. Both of these models incorporate the strength of the rotating bolt head and the aid of gas opera-tion. Since Franchi shotguns are essentially a division of Beretta Holding Corporation, Beretta factories in Italy and Spain produce the barrels for all of Franchi's shotguns. Beretta has a reputation for producing high-grade, chrome-lined shotgun barrels.

I have patterned several ver-sions of the Franchi 912 and find that they produce consist-ently tight patterns at turkey hunting ranges. Camouflaged, black synthetic and wood stocked models offer hunters a choice of styles to fit any turkey hunter's needs.

Semi-Auto 10 Gauges

Ithaca Mag 10

In 1974 Ithaca introduced the Mag-10 semi-automatic shot-gun. Weighing in at 11 pounds, this 3½-inch 10 gauge was a true stopper for waterfowl and turkey hunters. These guns were manufactured until 1986, when Ithaca fell on hard times. The company was purchased by Ithaca Acquisition Corporation in 1986 and continued opera-tion until sold to another party in 1996. Ithaca Acquisition Corporation sold the patent rights to Remington, which began production of the SP-10 model in 1989. Two years later, the SP-10 Turkey Combo was introduced. This combination package included an extra 22-inch barrel.

The Remington Model SP-10 Magnum is America's most popular gas-operated 10-gauge shotgun. At the heart of this autoloader is a corrosion-resistant gas system in which the cylinder–not the piston–moves to soften recoil. The SP-10 Magnum Camo features a new fast-pointing 26-inch vent rib barrel covered in

Mossy Oak Break-Up camouflage. It includes interchangeable Rem Chokes in Full and Modified and is supplied with sling swivel studs and a padded Cordura sling. The SP-10 weighs 10½ pounds.

Browning Gold 10

The entire Browning Gold Hunter series is built on a self-cleaning, gas-operated, short-stroke action. The 10-gauge version is offered with walnut stocks and matte or blued finish, or you can opt for the Gold Stalker series with a black synthetic stock. The Gold series was introduced in 1994, and the Gold Stalker series was launched in 1998. The guns are manufactured by Miroku in Japan and imported by Browning.

Semi-Auto 20 Gauges

Previously, I mentioned small-bore turkey guns. Their use covers a wide spectrum. Experienced turkey hunters are switching to lightweight guns and restricting the range at which they shoot birds. On the other hand, young or small-framed turkey hunters welcome the reduction in recoil.

The Benelli M1 Field 20 gauge offers a lightweight package in a top quality outfit. The same quality craftsmanship found in the Benelli Super Black Eagle is incorporated into the design of the M1 20 gauge. Three barrel lengths are offered: 24, 26 and 28 inches, each fitted with a stepped vent rib.

Browning Gold 20

The Browning Gold 20 is gas-operated, and follows the same design as its 12-gauge cousin. NWTF CEO Rob Keck has hunted several seasons with a Browning Gold 20 gauge. He carries a custom camouflaged version of this model while he carries out his hosting duties for the *Turkey Call* television show. The only disadvantage of this model is that it is not yet available in a camouflaged synthetic version.

Remington Model 1100

The Model 1100 Youth Synthetic Turkey Camo is an ideal choice for small-framed adults or young hunters. This 20-gauge lightweight autoloader balances a 1-inch shorter stock with a 21-inch vent rib barrel. Chambered for 20-gauge magnum shells, the gas-operated action reduces recoil. It is supplied with a Full Rem Choke tube that can be easily interchanged with other Rem Chokes. The synthetic stock and fore-end are covered with Realtree's Advantage camo, and both barrel and receiver have a non-reflective, black matte finish.

I have fired scores of test patterns with a 20-gauge Model 1100 and find that the best results are achieved with after-market choke tubes. Hastings and Colonial are my choice in the 1100, with magnum loads of No. 6 shot producing better patterns than larger sizes. This model is set up for heavy 3-inch shotshells and will not function well with target and field loads.

11. Pump-Action Shotguns

BENELLI NOVA PUMP 12-GAUGE

12-gauge Pump-Action Shotguns

Benelli Nova Pump 12-gauge

The Nova Pump represents a new way of building shotguns. Designed by Benelli's engineers in Urbino, Italy, the Nova doesn't use a conventional receiver and separate wooden buttstock. Instead, the Nova has a single unit that incorporates a light-but-rigid steel liner encased in a glass-reinforced thermopolymer shell, resulting in superior strength and corrosion resistance.

The buttstock has a recess for easy installation of an optional recoil reducer, a welcome accessory when heavy 3½-inch loads are selected. Getting to the recess is as easy as twisting off the recoil pad.

A button in the bottom of the fore-end activates a shell stop, allowing the chambered shell to be removed and preventing the next round from being released into the action.

Of particular interest to turkey hunters are the 24-inch barrel models in black matte synthetic and Advantage camo. Complementing the Nova's unique design and top-notch Benelli quality is its affordability.

Remington Model 870

No fewer than eight different Remington 870 models were cataloged in 2002. More than 2 million Model 870s have been produced since the gun was introduced in 1950. I have owned several 870s over the years, and my first turkey gun was an 870 that was originally fitted with a 28-inch vent rib barrel. I shipped the barrel to Nu-Line Guns in Harvester, Missouri, to have the barrel cut to 21 inches and threaded for choke tubes. This gun has accounted for scores of gobblers over the past few years.

Model 870 SPS-T
Super Magnum Camo CL

Fully camouflaged with Mossy Oak Break-Up, the Model 870 SPS-T Super Mag Camo has a durable synthetic Monte Carlo-style stock and fore-end with a vented recoil pad and 23-inch cantilever barrel, providing a heavy-duty base for scope installation. Furnished with a matching camouflaged padded sling and a Turkey Super Full Rem Choke, this gun is designed for optimal performance in any turkey-hunting situation. This gun tips the scales at 7½ pounds.

Model 870 SPS-T Super Magnum

The Model 870 SPS-T Super Magnum Camo is ideally designed for turkey hunting. It comes with a 3½-inch chambered, 23-inch vent rib barrel and integral Rem Choke system. Remington's Turkey Super Full and Extra Full choke tubes for exceptionally dense patterns are included. The relatively short barrel avoids catching overhead branches when the shotgun is slung over the shoulder, and it comes with an ivory front bead and steel mid-bead for quick, accurate sighting on the bobbing heads and necks of wary gobblers. The versatile Mossy Oak Break-Up camo pattern helps it blend into virtually any background. Sling swivels and studs are standard, and a matching, camo pattern Cordura sling is furnished.

Model 870 SPS-T Turkey Gun RS/TG

Providing turkey hunters with a wide range of options, Remington introduced two new Model 870 Special Purpose turkey guns in 2002, including a youth model. Both versions are available in 12 gauge and are fully camouflaged in the Mossy Oak Break-Up pattern. Each

REMINGTON 870 SPS-T TURKEY

REMINGTON 870 EXPRESS

model is equipped with swivel studs, swivels and padded sling.

Complete with a durable, fully-camouflaged synthetic stock, this 12-gauge pump-action shotgun has a 20-inch Rem Choke barrel (Turkey Super Full choke included) and Monte Carlo-style stock with vented recoil pad. The Model 870 SPS-T is also equipped with the TRUGLO light-gathering fiber-optic sight system. Frequent warranty repair returns for all the Remingtons fitted with TRUGLO sights will likely be the demise of these guns. Word on the street is that once standing orders are filled, Remington will cease production of TRUGLO- fitted models.

Model 870 Express Turkey

A perfect turkey gun with the concealment advantages of non-glare Express wood and metal finishes. Available in 12 gauge, with a 21-inch vent rib turkey barrel that carries easily beneath overhanging branches and minimizes movement on a stand. A turkey Extra Full Rem Choke tube provides the exceptionally dense patterns needed for taking a cautious tom.

Model 870 Express Turkey Camo

The synthetic stock and fore-end of the Model 870 Express Turkey gun are covered in Advantage camo to help hunters stay invisible to the prying eyes of a wary gobbler. Like all Express shotguns, it includes the concealment advantages of a non-reflective flat finish on exposed metal–available in 12 gauge, with 21-inch vent rib turkey barrel. An Extra Full Rem Choke tube provides the dense patterns necessary for effective coverage of the vital head and neck area of a big gobbler.

Model 870 Express Super Magnum Turkey Camo

Designed specifically for hunting the most suspicious, outer-fringe gobblers, the Model 870 Express Super Magnum Turkey Camo matches a 23-inch vent rib barrel and Turkey Extra Full Rem Choke with Advantage camo synthetic stock. Combined with 12-gauge, 3½-inch magnum turkey loads, it provides an extremely powerful turkey-hunting combination.

Model 870 Express Super Magnum SyntheticTurkey

The Model 870 Express Super Magnum Synthetic Turkey provides the heavy load capacity of 12-gauge, 3½-inch shells for turkey hunting at an affordable price. Simultaneously, it allows the optional flexibility of using any other 12-gauge loads in 3-inch or 2¾-inch shell lengths as well. The standard Turkey Extra Full Rem Choke delivers desirably dense patterns with all loads, and can be interchanged with other, more open Rem Chokes when appropriate. Fast pointing and precise sighting result from the 23-inch vent rib barrel with both ivory front and steel mid beads. And the black synthetic stock and matte black metal finish on barrel and receiver blend unobtrusively into any background.

Browning BPS Turkey Special Game Gun

South Carolina's 1993 Western Piedmont spring turkey season was rather frustrating for many hunters, and mine was no exception. As April closed, it looked as if the season would be a bust. The idea of not killing a gobbler wasn't nearly as bad as not even hearing a gobbler after the first week of the season. The last day of the Palmetto

A BROWNING BPS Turkey Special Game Gun was used to bag this late-season tom.

State's gobbler season fell on a Saturday, and I spent it hunting a large block of game management land on the Sumter National Forest. The day was also my last chance to bag a tom with Browning's BPS 12-gauge Turkey Special Game Gun before returning it to the manufacturer.

Just before the 1993 spring season began, I had gotten a call from Paul Thompson, Browning's press relations manager, who asked me to give the Turkey Special a thorough testing. I had put the scattergun through the ringer at the patterning board and found that it preferred Federal's Premier turkey load, a 3-inch magnum stuffed with 2 ounces of copper-plated No. 5s. At 40 yards, patterns hovered around 85percent with adequately dense centers. Fitted with a Browning Invector screw-in turkey tube, this particular gun also liked Remington's Duplex 4x6, 2-ounce loads and 2-ounce loads of No. 6 shot in Winchester's 3-inch magnum hulls.

I carried the short-barreled pump gun on several hunts, but fate never put a tom within range. The morning before the last day of the season found me listening to three mature birds sounding off from the roost. Duties at the office cut the

hunt short, but a brief long-distance encounter with one of the toms, displaying on a 100-acre burned cutover, gave me a clue as to how to set up the next morning.

At 6:30 a.m. I located one of the toms, roosted on the edge of the burn. Seconds after setting up, I caught a glimpse of the gobbler's silhouette as it glided down into the burned clearcut. After a few yelps, the mature tom responded; then a hen came onto the scene offering the tom things I couldn't deliver.

Three hours, two bred hens and five setups later, the tom went silent. Forty-five minutes later a gobble jarred me from a most restful nap. The tom had finally moved off the burn, allowing me to relocate for the sixth time that morning. By now he had become stubborn, only answering a

particular type of call only once. Finally, he answered a Rohm Brothers box call each time I yelped and cutt to him. He started moving away again, so I set up closer to where he had last gobbled. This cat-and-mouse game continued until 12:45 p.m., and he hadn't responded in 45 minutes.

Enough was enough. I packed it in, and wouldn't you know, he gobbled from my last position when I had walked about 300 yards. The foliage allowed me to close the gap to 150 yards. After several minutes the bearded one sounded off, and it seemed that he was moving away again. I got up and moved toward him along an old roadbed, lined on one side with poison ivy-covered, century-old oaks. Suddenly, the tom thundered from about 75 yards away. The only choice I had for a quick setup was the closest ivy-cloaked oak. I yelped twice with the box call to give the tom a bearing.

Then things really got interesting. My hasty choice of setup disturbed the clump of ivy's legless tenant. Not wanting to move and chance scaring the tom, I gritted my teeth as a 4-foot-long black snake slithered across the toe of my right boot. Seconds later the tom broke into full strut 50 yards in the heart of a thicket directly to the front. Soft purring with a double-reeded diaphragm pulled him out of his strut and at long last started him in the right direction. Thumbing the Browning's tang safety off as the bird advanced was satisfying, to say the least. He finally cleared the thicket at 12 yards and caught a 2-ounce swarm of Federal No. 5s, ending the hunt just over seven hours after it started.

Beyond being a proven turkey taker, the Browning BPS Turkey Special Game Gun also carries well. Its compact overall length is complemented with a relatively-balanced feel. The barrel measures 20½-inches, which make its 40⅞-inch overall length handy in thick cover situations. Its walnut stocks are appropriately non-glare satin-finished walnut and its metal finish is likewise dull to retard light reflection that can spook a keen-eyed tom in a heartbeat.

That turkey season wasn't my first experience with Browning's pump shotgun. Gene Wood, the father of one of my high-school friends, Jerry, loaned me a BPS for an entire fall hunting season several years back. That gun, as well as the Turkey Special I recently tested, offer a quality fit and finish. An added touch of class is the engraved game scene depicted on the sides of the receiver.

Rigged for a detachable sling, the Turkey Special comes equipped with an adjustable web sling. Tipping the scales at 7 pounds, 7 ounces, the Turkey Special falls into a weight range that is comfortable to carry on long hunts.

Some of the features of the BPS include bottom ejection and a top tang safety, which makes it ideal for both right-handed and southpaw shooters.

The stock dimensions for the Game Gun were devised with deer and turkey hunters in mind. The length of pull measures 13⅞-inches, slightly shorter than the wing shooter's BPS model. Its shorter butt stock makes it easier to shoulder quickly when wearing thick clothing during deer

THE MOSSBERG 835 led the 3 ½-inch magnum 12-gauge revolution.

55

season. Turkey hunters will find that its shorter length is well suited for shooting from the sitting position, too. The drop at comb and drop at heel both measure 1½ inches, which give this shotgun rifle-like proportions. Fitted with standard rifle sights, this gun was meant to be aimed rather than pointed. The gun's receiver is drilled and tapped for scope mounting for those who prefer finer optics. Shell capacity is five 2¾-inch or 3-inch shells, which includes one in the chamber.

After taking all manner of small game and big game with a BPS, I recommend it highly for those hunters who like pump-action shotguns.

Mossberg 500 12 gauge

If you are searching for a budget priced turkey gun, you might consider the Mossberg 500. Several versions are offered in adult and youth sizes. The models fitted for screw-in choke tubes will accept Winchoke-style chokes.

Mossberg 835 3½-inch 12-gauge

This is the gun that started the 3½-inch 12-gauge revolution. Instead of bringing a new 10-gauge waterfowl gun to market in the late 1980s, the New Haven, Connecticut arms maker teamed up with Federal Cartridge to create the first production gun for the then-new powerhouse 3½-inch 12-gauge waterfowl loads. The Mossberg 835 has been offered in several configurations since it was first introduced in 1989.

Currently, the Mossberg 835 turkey guns are offered in three camouflage patterns: Advantage Timber, Realtree Hardwoods and O. F. Mossberg's own version of a woodland pattern. Stocks are synthetic, with the exception of a turkey and deer combo. Turkey hunting models include ported, 24-inch vent-ribbed barrels fitted with fiber-optic sights. If you are considering an 835 Ulti-Mag, the Dual-Comb stock offered in the Turkey Combo will be your best choice if you plan to mount a scope. The raised comb is better suited for scope use, and you'll get a rifled slug barrel for the same price as one of the Advantage or Realtree turkey models.

Ithaca's Model 37 Featherweight

Pump-action shotguns have long been my favorite. I fondly recall coming in from school on the opening day of dove season. Finding that long, brown cardboard box lying in the middle of the den floor was the biggest surprise of my young life. The most memorable gift before or since, the Savage 12-gauge pump set the stage for my preference for hunting with a slick slide-action.

In the years since, when I've hunted with a Model 37 Ithaca pump, I've always enjoyed the light weight, feel and fit. A few years ago, Ithaca fell on tough times. A new owner and a scaled-

ITHACA TURKEYSLAYER

down product line focusing on the Model 37 Featherlight have the venerable company back on the track to providing hunters with quality firearms.

A couple of years ago, Ithaca expanded their Model 37 versions to include the Turkeyslayer version. The first two years' Turkeyslayers had camouflaged wood stocks, improved sights and was threaded for screw-in choke tubes. Further refining the Model 37 for serious turkey hunters' needs, Ithaca made several improvements that are evident when you pull the trigger.

Starting with the trigger, the 1999 models have one of the best let-offs offered on a factory shotgun. It's crisp, has little creep, and when coupled with a set of TRUGLO rifle sights, helps keep you on target when sending a tight-shooting turkey load down range.

The first Model 37 I shot years ago could "kick the shortening out of a biscuit" with magnum loads. The Model 37's reputation as a lightweight and a sharp drop in the butt stock dimensions contributed to its reputation as a gun that would kick. Some welcome improvements make it easier on the shoulder and the shooter's cheek. New in 2000 was a synthetic stock, which had less drop and a higher comb height. The new stock dimensions translate into less felt recoil with powerful turkey loads. I was pleasantly surprised when I touched off the first round during an afternoon-long patterning session. I expected to get walloped, but didn't feel any worse for the wear at the end of the day's shooting. Although still a lightweight, these guns are a few ounces heavier than older versions, tipping the scales at 7 pounds, 5 ounces. The few extra ounces also add to the gun's lighter felt recoil.

Other improvements that reduce recoil and produce better patterns are the barrel's lengthened forcing cone. The 22-inch barrel is also threaded for Winchoke-type threads, and comes from the factory with a Colonial Arms extended choke tube measures .665 diameter, and has 61 points of constriction when compared to the Model 37's .726 bore diameter.

A good measure of performance for any turkey gun is how many pellets strike inside a 10-inch circle at 40 yards. Several different turkey loads were tested on NWTF targets. The three Model 37s that were tested had a distinct preference for Winchester Supreme High-Velocity 3-inch magnums loaded with 1¾-ounces of No. 6 shot. Every other load tested yielded about half the number of shots inside a 10-inch circle in comparison to these loads. The average number of pellets inside the 10-inch ring was 87, with the best pattern showing 104 pellet holes. The average number pellets in the turkey's head and neck area averaged 24. This combination of gun

ITHACA'S 37 16-gauge rifle-sighted model is a special-order gun.

and load combination should be "lights out" for gobblers at 40 yards.

A variety of camouflage patterns are offered on the Model 37 Turkeyslayer. The guns tested were wearing Realtree Hardwoods, with Advantage, Realtree X-Tra Brown and X-Tra Gray also offered as finish options.

A couple of years ago, Ithaca began once again chambering their Model 37 pump guns in 16 gauge. These guns are special-order affairs, which has limited their numbers. Out of curiosity, and a bit of nostalgia, I asked Robin Sharpless, Ithaca's new publicity man, if it would be possible to create a 16-gauge turkey gun. We discussed how to set up the gun, and whether to fit it with a fancy camo job. Wanting to keep a more traditional look, I opted for a non-reflective matte blue finish for the metal and a hand-rubbed stock. True to his word, Robin had the craftsmen at Ithaca bob the barrel to 22 inches, mount rifle sights and thread it for a screw-in Colonial Arms choke. Although it wasn't necessary,

the lightweight 16 gauge also got a barrel porting job.

As luck would have it, I hunted with the Ithaca several times last spring, but never got a chance to kill a gobbler. The one-of-a-kind turkey gun would have done well enough, if given the chance. I patterned it with two custom Nitro loads, which did well for shots 25 yards and closer. These loads consisted of 1⅛ ounces of No. 5 or No. 6 shot. I also shot several test patterns with Winchester Super X 6 shot loads. These performed well enough to stretch the maximum range to 30 yards.

Winchester Model 1300

The legendary firearms manufacturer offers a solid pump-action that rivals the popularity of the Remington 870. Winchester has manufactured several Model 1300 versions with the turkey hunter in mind. Its 6-pound, 6-ounce weight is ideal for comfortable carrying. The first Model 1300 turkey gun was offered between 1985 and 1988. The Win-Cam version, offered between 1987 and 1993, fea-

tured a greenish laminated stock. In 1989 Winchester introduced the 1300 Win-Cam NWTF (National Wild Turkey Federation) series I-IV, which was discontinued in 1994. These models were fitted with various sight combinations. The most recent version has synthetic stocks and a black matte finish.

New for 2002, Winchester offered the Model 1300 with a compact 18-inch barrel and a new Extra-long, Extra-full extended turkey tube. Featuring a rugged composite stock and forearm, this version is fully covered in Mossy Oak Break-Up camo. A magazine cap and stock sling studs are standard, as are the adjustable TRUGLO fiber-optic sights. The receiver is drilled and tapped for mounting a scope or red-dot type sight. "Team NWTF" is printed on the butt stock.

After countless hours at the range and in the field with a Model 1300, I give it high marks. Following is a story from

THE WINCHESTER 1300 12-gauge is a dependable performer on wild turkeys.

58

a 1992 issue of *Turkey Call* magazine in which I put a Model 1300 to good use on a North Carolina hunt.

"Some Things Are Worth the Wait."

Anticipation seems to be a dying art in today's hurry-up world. In the form of an emotion, it's the feelings a small boy endured when Mom laid out a pan of piping hot sourdough biscuits to cool. Mouth watering, the youngster thought he would be grown and off to college before she would slice and spread a dollop of butter on the first one. Small, grasping hands outstretched, feet shuffling on cold linoleum, Mom's little man knew the wait was almost over when she took the milk bottle out of the Frigidaire. It's funny how mothers know that waiting for something special is half the treat.

And something special was in the making again. A month of long days and late nights sitting in front of a computer terminal was over. The caller was off to the printer, and it was time to take a weekend off to recharge the spirit and rest the eyes.

Car loaded with hunting and fishing gear, the miles melted away touring the back roads and less-traveled paths through South Carolina and Georgia on the way to a special place nestled in the mountains of North Carolina. Beckoned by a friend for a few days of turkey hunting and trout fishing, the childlike feelings of anticipation rose with every click of the odometer.

This odyssey was born in a cold month, and matured with the changing of seasons. Telephone conversations with Jim Casada, writer, scholar, and, most of all, turkey hunter from South Carolina, laid the foundation for a trip that would produce both tom turkeys and mountain trout. Jim spun a convincing yarn of past days spent wading creeks and climbing ridges to get above the longbeards living in the Nantahala National Forest. He also told of climbing back down those same ridges at the morning's end, pausing to study those same creeks, not as a turkey hunter's obstacle as before, but as a fisherman.

Enough's enough. This sportsman was ready

Hunting the North Carolina mountains for spring gobblers often requires lots of climbing and an occasional cooling dip. The author's tom proved no different.

to sleep on a cold, wet creek rock just to get a chance at this adventure. But Jim assured me that our accommodations would rank with the finest. We would be the guests of Roy and Kathy Wilson, owners of Blue Boar Lodge.

Nearing journey's end, I stopped in Robbinsville, North Carolina, to get directions out to the lodge. Back on the road, a short winding trip up and around two arms of the starfish-shaped Lake Santeetla brought me to my destination.

Upon arrival I was greeted by guide Ricky Walls, just in from a successful day's hunt in the national forest. Introduced to some of the other guests and Ricky's proud sport, I was enthralled with the hunter's story of the tom's undoing.

A clanking supper chime signaled that it was time to stow baggage and answer the call. Kathy made a feast of venison steaks, mashed potatoes, gravy, greens, and, wouldn't you know, homemade biscuits. I had good feelings about this place.

Once the meal was over, it was time to plan a strategy to locate a gobbler. All options considered, Ricky decided to match wits with The Horse Cove Gobbler.

Next morning began with the host's solid rapping on my bedroom's chestnut door. Stepping into the lodge's dimly lit hallway, the senses were greeted with the familiar aroma of a Southern hunting camp breakfast: grits, eggs, bacon—and you guessed it—steamy homemade biscuits. After the third cup of coffee, it was time to go.

A short drive to the head of Horse Cove Trail, then a mile climb, brought Ricky and his hunter to the haunts of the trail's long-bearded namesake. Pausing, four of the senses seemed sharper in the tomblike darkness. The absence of sight let the mind paint a vivid picture of why one hunts turkeys in the spring.

The smell of rhododendron and fern mingled with rotting leaves and moss brushed the mental canvas with wide, dark strokes. The odor of unknown wildflowers rose up to add the brighter hues in this masterpiece of the mind. Turning to face the gentle breeze, the skin was kissed with the coolness of a smooth mountain mist, condensing, trickling down, mingling with sweat from the toil of the journey to be tasted on parched lips. Add to these the steady spattering of heavy dew

and the gurgling of a brook, now suddenly interrupted by the wild turkey's call, and the mural became complete.

We heard another faint gobble, barely audible over cascading Horse Cove Creek, allowing us to course the bird. Still more climbing was called for, so we waded the creek and began our assault on the valley's southwest wall. Leaning into the mountain, our climb was aided by sapling handholds and louder gobbling as we worked to get into position. Safely above our quarry, we chose an ancient white oak straddling a finger ridge for our setup. A few whispered words and Ricky turned to find his hiding spot 30 yards to the rear, ready to lend a few yelps on his box call if the gobbler got hung up. Scooping out a seat in the moldy forest litter, I eased down and loosened the bindings on a new knee brace (acquired after tearing a ligament three weeks before) to assure good circulation and prevent an untimely leg cramp. Gun resting on the good knee, calls in place, the stage was set for spring's finest show.

Tree yelps made with a Roy Rhodes cocobolo striker on an H. S. Strut slate were answered with a lusty limb rattle from the bird's roost in the valley below. A few moments later he voiced his claim to the mountain, goaded on by a few sleepy crows. The sun threw a silvery cast on the overcast skies, signaling that legal shooting time had come. Taking hat in hand, I flapped it against my pant leg

while giving a poor imitation of a hen's fly-down cackle. But love is blind, or, in this case, deaf, because the tom double-gobbled to the false hen's clamoring.

All this noise didn't set too well with the pileated woodpecker sleeping in the hollow tree overhead. He poked his head out and let out a stream of avian swears that would have made a New York City cab driver blush, which were answered by another double gobble. This chain reaction of bird talk, sparked by rubbing stick on slate rock, electrified the woods as other fowl added their voices.

Then all was quiet. Suddenly, powerful wingbeats carried the longbeard up the valley. Wings set, his black silhouette glided silently above the treetops below, burning an indelible image on my brain. Screened by the foliage on the finger ridge paralleling mine, the gobbler touched down, unseen, unheard. Shifting the Winchester 1300 slightly to the right and releasing the safety, I waited. Then he was there, head glowing neon white. Instead of coming in full strut, the tom came in silently, pacing his advance, looking for his hen. Advancing a step at a time, the gobbler walked down into the depression, my gunsight riveted to his wattles. Still closing the gap at 40 yards, my confidence rose, until he paused at 25 yards to receive a Double XX engraved, copper-plated invitation to supper.

At the blast, Ricky was up and racing past me to secure the bird as I gingerly hobbled and slid down the slope on one good leg. Hunt over, we savored the moment, admiring our trophy. Examining both beard and spurs, which were later measured at 9¹²⁄₁₆ inches and ¹⁵⁄₁₆ inch, respectively, we speculated as to whether this was the same bird that had given him fits of frustration all season. Owing to the gobbler's silent approach once on the ground, and since Ricky had heard another turkey farther up the valley shock-gobble at the gunshot, we decided it would remain a mystery until Jim Casada could join us for a hunt the following morning.

Knee brace cinched down and game shouldered, we made our way back down the mountain, discussing plans for tomorrow's hunt. The day was far from over. It could be spent casting for native brook trout in the higher elevations or chasing browns and rainbows in the bigger runs below. Soon Jim arrived at camp and we set off for nearby streams, where we added brookies, 'bows and browns to the day's bag.

The last morning of the season, Jim and I returned to Horse Cove but were unable to locate more than one lone hen amid sporadic downpours. Everything dampened but our resolve, we promised to return again some day to solve the mystery of The Horse Cove Gobbler. What's more, it left me with yet another adventure to plan and anticipate during the idle times, and even though it would be another year before I could return, some things are worth the wait.

10-Gauge Pump Shotguns

The Browning BPS Stalker and Magnum hunter are the only 10 gauge pump guns currently manufactured. The BPS Stalker is offered in black synthetic and matte-finished metal. A camouflaged version is offered in Mossy Oak Shadow Grass, but is typically available in the longer barrel lengths that work better in duck blinds than in woodland hunting applications. This model, as well as many other Browning models, are manufactured by Miroku in Japan for importation by Browning.

20-Gauge Pump Shotguns

Benelli Nova

Benelli introduced the Nova 20 gauge in 2001, and added a camouflaged version the following year. A 20-gauge Nova dressed in Advantage Timber High Definition offers a dependable, stealthy gun at an affordable price. Barrel lengths available are 28, 26 and 24 inches. A mercury recoil reducer is available as an option.

Model 870 Express Youth Turkey Camo

For young or smaller-framed hunters who want a hardworking turkey gun tailored just for their needs, Remington offers the Model 870 Express Youth Turkey gun with a 1-inch shorter synthetic stock and fore-end covered in Advantage camo. This 20 gauge Express comes with a 21-inch vent rib turkey barrel and a full Rem Choke tube.

I have owned a non-camouflaged 870 Youth version for several years. This gun has accounted for several gobblers in the hands of novice hunters both young and old. I get the most consistent patterns from 3-inch, 1½-ounce loads of No. 6 shot. My choke of choice has been a Colonial in the XF constriction. Although some might get better performance from tighter choke constrictions, this particular gun dislikes overlytight chokes with turkey loads.

Mossberg 500 20 Gauge

If you are searching for a budget-priced turkey gun, you might consider the Mossberg 500. Several versions in 20 gauge are offered in adult and youth sizes. The models fitted for screw-in choke tubes will accept Win Choke-style chokes.

16-Gauge Pump Shotguns

Ithaca Model 37

This century-old arms maker was resurrected by Ithaca Acquisition Corp. in 1986, and has focused manufacturing on the Model 37. Limited custom-ordered Model 37 16 gauges are once again available. The shorter barrel

REMINGTON'S 870 20-gauge youth version is a good bet for small-framed hunters.

lengths are suitable for turkey hunting. I custom- ordered a 16 gauge smoothbore Deer-slayer version, which accepts choke tubes and is fitted with fiber-optic rifle sights. It is a pleasure to carry and patterns well out to 30 yards.

Model 870 16 gauge

Absent from the lineup since 1980, Remington brought back the 16-gauge shotgun in four variations of the Model 870. Long a favorite of the target and wing-shooter, the 16 gauge offers ballistically-balanced performance and milder recoil.

Model 870 Wingmaster

This Model 870 Wingmaster is built on the same frame as the original 16-gauge Wingmaster, allowing for parts to be interchanged. This traditional beauty combines a high-gloss, American walnut stock and fore-end with polished, blued-metal work and a non-embellished receiver. Available in 28-inch or 26-inch light contour, vent rib Rem Choke barrel.

Model 870 Express

Considered the workhorse of pump-action shotguns, the Model 870 Express combines a sturdy hardwood stock and fore-end with a rugged, durable black oxide metal finish. The 28-inch light contour vent rib barrel comes with a Modified Rem Choke tube and has a single front bead sight.

Model 870 Express Synthetic

When harsh conditions are the forecast for the day, the Model 870 Express Synthetic lives up to the task. With all the standard features of the Express 16 gauge, this version adds a strong, weather-resistant black synthetic stock and fore-end.

Model 870 Express Synthetic Youth

The 16 gauge is the ideal choice for youth or smaller stature shooters with its milder recoil and performance capabilities. The Model 870 Express Synthetic Youth in 16 gauge features a 23-inch light contour vent rib barrel with Modified Rem Choke and "youth" stock that is 1 inch shorter than the standard Model 870.

For added versatility, Remington's complete line of Model 870 Rem Choke Extra barrels will fit older versions of the 16-gauge Model 870 shotguns. Big Green's reintroduction of the 16-gauge warms my heart. Fond memories of my earliest hunts when I carried a 16-gauge guarantee that I'll put one of these in the hands of my sons. I hope that the advances in turkey ammunition seen in 10-, 12- and 20-gauge loads are transferred to new 16-gauge fodder.

12. One Shot or Two: Single-Barrel and Double-Barrel Turkey Guns

A tight-choked single-shot can make a handy turkey gun. Its simplistic design and light weight work well for the rookie as well as the veteran turkey hunter. One of the most functional single-shots I have seen is a customized Winchester Model 37. This gun had extensive barrel work and was re-choked to throw ultra-dense patterns by Ye Olde Gunsmith in Missouri. More than one million Winchester Model 37s were produced between 1936 and 1963, so it might be rather easy to find one in a local pawnshop and find a reputable gunsmith to create your own version.

Single-Shots

New England Firearms

New England Firearms and its subsidiary Harrington & Richardson offer a variety of affordable single-shots chambered in 10, 12, 16, 20, and 28 gauge and .410 bore. The models seeing the most use for turkey hunting are the 3½-inch-chambered 10 and 12 gauge. Several thousand youth model 20 gauges have been put in the hands of new shooters as well. Mossy Oak camouflage and screw-in choke tubes accessorize the 24-inch barreled versions.

Mossberg

Mossberg's SSi-One Turkey Shotgun is a single-shot, lever-opening, break action design with 3½-inch-chambered 12 gauge with a 24-inch over-bored, ported barrel and extended Ulti-full Turkey Choke Tube. This model includes matte metal finish, fluted, cut-checkered, satin-finished black walnut stock and fore-end; swivel posts for quick-disconnect sling swivels, top tang safety, cocking indicator and scope base.

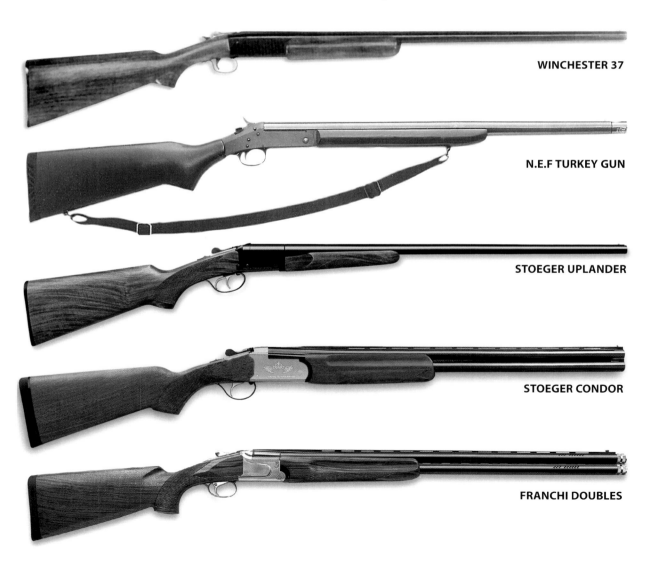

WINCHESTER 37

N.E.F TURKEY GUN

STOEGER UPLANDER

STOEGER CONDOR

FRANCHI DOUBLES

Stoeger

The rugged Stoeger Single Barrel Shotgun features a transfer bar, cross-bolt safety and a break-open design operated by the trigger guard. The barrels are designed for screw-in chokes and are available in 12 and 20 gauge.

Double Barrel

Quite a few turkey hunters go afield with double-barreled scatterguns each season. A smattering of over-and-under and side-by-side models have been designed specifically for turkey hunting. The few models designated as turkey guns have been discontinued due to slow sales. One of the few turkey hunting-specific double-barrel side-by-sides was the NWTF 10-gauge commemorative imported by American Arms in 1985. Most any of the double barrels in production today can be pressed into service as a functional gobbler getter. Quite a few twin- bore fans will read this and think otherwise, but the vast array of other action types better serve today's turkey hunter.

Stoeger

The Uplander, a traditional double-trigger side-by-side, is produced in 12 and 20 gauge and handles 3-inch ammunition. The Uplander is available with screw-in interchangeable choke tubes. The Short Stock Uplander, with a 13-inch length-of-pull, is an excellent choice for women or junior shooters.

Over-Under

Franchi

The Alcione SL Sport over-and-under is manufactured with a 30-inch ported barrel, extended knurled choke tubes, and is chambered for 2¾-inch target loads.

The Alcione line of guns features a full range of interchangeable barrels in 20 and 12 gauge. The Veloce, meaning "fast" in Italian, weighs only 5½ pounds and is available in 20 and 28 gauge built on a shallow aluminum alloy receiver. A steel insert in the breech face adds strength for magnum loads. Barrel selection is accomplished by setting the tang-mounted safety lever for the desired firing sequence. The barrels have 3-inch chambers in 20 gauge, and 2¾-inch chambers in 28 gauges. They are chrome-lined for increased durability.

THIS AMERICAN Arms 12-gauge over- and-under was an NWTF Trade Gun in 1996 and 1997.

IV. Turkey Gun Tune-Ups

The starting point for improving your turkey gun is to work on the barrel. Patterning various loads starts the process. Once you've found how the gun performs, then you can try various techniques to raise its patterning effectiveness, as well as adding custom features that fit your individual taste. Minor modifications and shooting technique will reduce recoil, too.

13. Fine Tuning Your Turkey Gun: Muzzle to Chamber

> "Changing loads from one brand to the next can change the point of impact downrange. Switching choke tubes can change point of impact, too."

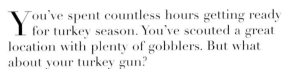

You've spent countless hours getting ready for turkey season. You've scouted a great location with plenty of gobblers. But what about your turkey gun?

There are some very important aspects of shooting a turkey gun accurately that need your attention before the season rolls around. After you've found a load that patterns well–one that will put over 100 pellets in a 10-inch circle at 40 yards–it's time to do some fine tuning.

When you're shooting a tight-patterning shotgun at a small target–like a gobbler's head and neck–you have to be sure the core of the load is hitting precisely where you aim.

Just like when shooting a rifle, changing loads from one brand to the next can change the point of impact downrange. Switching choke tubes can change point of impact, too.

I have found that 40 yards is the optimal range for testing the performance of turkey loads. A range setup comprised of a sturdy bench or other rest and a target frame about three feet square is essential. Several years ago the Winchester ammunition company offered a patterning target with several overlapping 30-inch circles printed around a drawing of a gobbler's head and neck. Though they are hard to find these days, these targets are the best I've ever seen for the primary stages of shotgun pattern testing. If you can't find the Winchester targets begin you shooting session by taping two full sheets of newspaper together to give you an area that will allow you to draw a 30-inch circle. Whichever target you use, the

PRESEASON PATTERNING sessions lay the foundation for successful hunts.

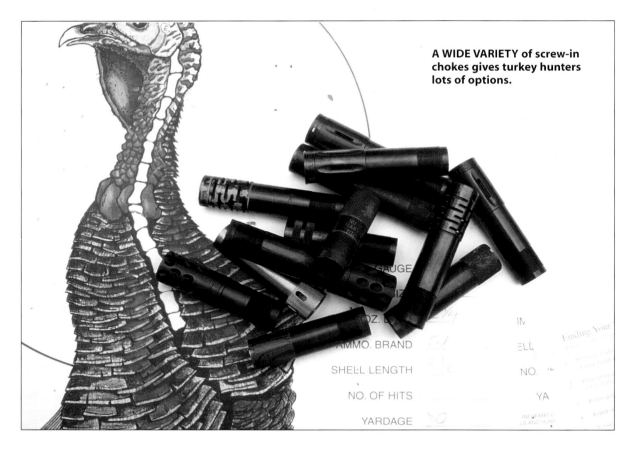

A WIDE VARIETY of screw-in chokes gives turkey hunters lots of options.

results will be the same. With the target in place mark a center aiming point; take careful aim and fire.

Shooting at a large target will tell you more about where your gun is shooting than smaller targets can reveal. Targets such as the National Wild Turkey Federation's official Still-Target work well for fine tuning, but are not large enough to register the entire pattern. Seeing where the entire pattern strikes is essential to telling if your gun and load combination is putting every shot where you aim. Multiple shots at new targets will minimize any human error in your testing.

Prior to the convenience of a backyard range, I frequented a public range on the Sumter National Forest near Edgefield, South Carolina. A new Browning turkey gun arrived for testing a few days prior to turkey season, so I was obliged to join several other turkey hunters as they patterned their gun at the range. One chap, who was suffering from the recoil produced by his Mossberg 835 12 gauge, decided that shooting from one of the available

benches was more than he could endure. After the first shot he stood and fired his gun off-hand to pattern and sight in his shotgun. To his chagrin, he did little more than put shots all over the paper. I learned the hard way that shooting from a bench is not the only way to test a heavy kicking gun. A tall camera tripod is the next best thing to a benchrest. I tape a piece of foam padding to the tripod head to cushion the gun and shoot from a standing position. Recoil is more tolerable when shooting from a standing position. Taking pity on the fellow turkey hunter, I walked to my truck and returned with my slightly modified camera tripod. I loaned the fellow my "standing bench" and he finished his patterning and sighting-in session with success.

Over the past several years I have found that about half of the turkey guns I fire don't place the center of the better-patterning loads where the gun is aimed. Determining where the fault lies starts with your shooting form.

Consistency is the key, so if your turkey gun has bead sights, make sure you go through a

AFTER-MARKET CHOKES come in constrictions from .640 to .690 for many 12-gauge barrel types.

mental checklist every time you get ready to shoot:

- Face tight to the stock every time
- Beads in perfect alignment
- Your shooting eye focused on the front sight, which should slightly blur the target.

Essentially, your eye is the back sight when using bead sights, so cheeking the gun the same way every time is just as important for turkey hunters and Olympic trap competitors alike. Following this regimen will give you quicker, more successful results when collecting shooting data, too.

The last steps in your preparation should include a shooting session where you are dressed in the garb and gear you plan to use on a hunt. Wear hunting clothes to make sure the gun fits the same way it does in the field. Also, if you plan to wear a face mask, shoot with in place, too. Try a few shots from a sitting position with the gun propped on your knee to make sure your eye–your rear sight–is lining up

the same as it did from a shooting bench.

Turkey hunters wishing to raise the performance of their favorite turkey gun have a long list of optional after-market accessories, or more sophisticated tune-ups better left to a qualified gunsmith. Some of these gunsmithing techniques include altering the internal dimensions of factory barrels to improve pattern performance. Choke tube selection is the simplest and most often tried method for tightening shot patterns by the do-it-yourself crowd.

Picking the right choke tube

During the 1990s, a host of companies in the hunting industry introduced hundreds of new extended, screw-in chokes with the turkey hunter in mind. A wide range of muzzle constrictions, coupled with unique designs can make choke tube selection a daunting task.

Today's turkey guns are specifically designed to shoot heavy payloads and give tight, dense patterns. To get the best performance from lead turkey loads, you need an extra-tight choke. And, to get the best performance from your gun, you may need to experiment with various choke sizes, designs and loads.

The extended screw-in chokes of today do more than give you a quick-change choice. The extended part of the tube typically includes a gradual constriction from the bore that is followed by a straight parallel section with a more tightly constricted muzzle. Obviously, the constricted parts of the choke work like a funnel to create a fine stream of shot. The straight section of the choke has an important job, too. The straight, or parallel, has a stabilizing effect on the shot string, which creates a more uniform pattern. Pattern uniformity is as critical to the turkey hunter as a tight pattern.

A normal 12-gauge barrel measures about .724 thousands of an inch. By comparison, a factory full choke squeezes down the muzzle to about .700 of an inch. The normal way to get tighter patterns is to reduce the choke size even more. For example, my Winchester 1300 likes a turkey choke that measures .665, and shoots No. 5 or 6 shot well.

You can have too much of a good thing. If you use a choke that's too tight for your gun and load, too much constriction has the tendency of creating ragged patterns with large holes.

Looking back several years to the predecessors of today's "turkey tubes," card shooters relied on 12-gauge choke constrictions of .640 and smaller to put at least one pellet dead center of an "X" marked target. The problem posed by using these super-tight constrictions is that they many times deform lead pellets and cause other disruptions in pattern performance. Though these small constrictions may consistently put a few pellets dead center, a large percentage of the pattern may fall outside a critical 10-inch circle at 40 yards. It also may create ragged voids between pellet holes. This can spell trouble for a turkey hunter trying to make a clean, killing shot on a gobbler. On the other hand, I have found a very few 12-gauge guns that perform well with these diminutive chokes when shooting No. 6 shot.

A good place to start with a standard-sized 12-gauge barrel is to try a .660 tube. Depending on the ammo, you may want to vary choke tube constriction to a tighter .655, a .650, or go in the other direction to a .665 or .670 tube. Since back-bored 12-gauge barrels measure as large as a 10 gauge, they usually do well with chokes that measure correspondingly larger. The most common back-bored 12 gauge turkey guns are Brownings and Winchesters with Invector Plus barrels, and Mossberg 835 Ulti-Mags. Beretta finally introduced a back-bored 12 gauge in 2001 with the Extrema.

A good starting point in selecting a choke for a back-bored barrel is a constriction measuring approximately .680 thousands of an inch. I have found that constrictions as small as .670 can produce good patterns with No. 5 or No. 6 shot from a Winchester Super X2. The smaller constriction tends to perform better when shooting the high-velocity 1¼-ounce loads from Federal or Winchester. Heavier 2-ounce loads typically prefer .680 to .690 chokes.

Following are some observations I've made over the years testing various chokes. These are not hard-and-fast rules, but merely my thoughts on their performance.

A WIDE VARIETY of chokes is available for nearly every shotgun model.

THE BENEFIT of vented chokes over non-vented makes is still debated.

Ballistic Specialties–The folks at Ballistic Specialties do a fine job of barrel work as well a producing top-notch chokes. I had a Remington 870 12-gauge barrel reworked by Ballistic Specialties and it improved pattern performance on an average of 10 percent. National Wild Turkey Federation national board member Gene Denton shared some of his experience with a BSI barrel job. Shooting Federal 2-ounce loads at 30-inch paper circles at 40 yards, Gene put 397 pellets (88.2 percent) in a 30-inch circle with No. 6s; 270 (79.4 percent) in a 30-inch circle with No. 5s; and 256 (94.8 percent) with No. 4 shot. Any pattern higher than 90 percent is a thing of beauty to be cherished by any turkey hunter. I've seen very few turkey guns that will actually print 40-yard patterns that average higher than 90%.

COMP-N-CHOKE *(top)*, Gobblin' Thunder *(center)* and Mad Max *(bottom)* chokes are the most popular tubes, even though other designs can provide tight patterns as well.

Briley–They've been in the business for quite a while. A wide range of tubes are available to fit most popular shotgun brands.

Browning Invector–These chokes have the same thread pattern as a WinChoke or Mossberg's 500 and 9200. These were the earliest vented chokes I experimented with back in the mid 1980s. Several pattern sessions led me to believe that the ports didn't really help all that much.

Browning Invector Plus–These are the back-bored Browning, and more recently, Winchester Super X2 sized chokes. Factory chokes have not fared as well as aftermarket chokes.

Carlson's–These are some of my favorite chokes. I had excellent luck with a Mossberg 9200 fitted with a .660 Carlson's tube. This gun and choke combination really like Winchester Hi-Velocity, 3-inch loaded with No. 5 shot. This gun typically puts more than 90 percent of these aforementioned loads inside a 30-inch circle at 40 yards.

Colonial–The Colonial chokes I've tested in 20 gauge really shine with the smaller shot sizes. I've got a Remington 1100 20 gauge that will print patterns in the low 80 percent range at 40 yards with 3-inch Federal No. 6 shot. The same choke, an XF, does well in a youth-model 870.

Comp-N-Choke–A wide range of constriction sizes for all major shotgun manufacturers make Comp-N-Choke one of my top choices for aftermarket tubes. No matter what gun or load I am testing, one of their tubes has consistently produced tight patterns. It's no wonder that Comp-N-Choke has won its share of NWTF sanctioned still-target competitions.

Gobblin' Thunder–The fact that Comp-N-Choke has built this brand of chokes since their first introduction gives some insight as to why they have performed so well in still-target competitions.

Hastings–Offers full range of chokes to fit proprietary Hastings barrels. Of special note is Hastings' Wadlock barrels, which are straight rifled to prevent the shot cup from spinning. This will enhance down-range performance by 3 percent to 10 percent.

H.S. Strut Under Taker–Another choice option for improving your turkey gun's performance. These tubes are offered to fit most popular shotguns. H.S. Strut's new combination front sight and choke tube is an interesting concept that works.

Lohman Long Shot–These tubes are relatively new on the turkey hunting scene. I have fired a few promising patterns with these tubes using a Winchester 1300 and a Remington 11-87 12 gauge.

M.A.D. Mad Max–Mark Drury wasn't quite satisfied with the chokes he relied on each spring, so he designed and introduced a full line of parallel ported tubes.

Mossberg–Factory tubes have included extended, ported types to improve turkey gun performance. These tubes consistently perform at levels below other specialty aftermarket tubes.

Nu-Line Guns–This gunsmithing company from Harvester, Missouri, produced the first turkey-hunting specific choke tubes that I've had

PATTERNMASTER chokes *(far left)* use a unique choking system that relies more on wad retention than tighter muzzle diameters. Nu-line *(right)* has been in the after-market choke business since the mid-1980s.

experience using. My first turkey gun was a Remington 870 that was cut down to 21 inches and threaded for WinChoke tubes. The hybrid combination has accounted for quite a few longbeards over the past two decades.

Patternmaster–The most recent advancements in choke design are drastic deviations from standard muzzle-constriction choke tubes. Patternmaster tubes have been popular for waterfowl shooters since the mid-'90s for their ability to pattern well with steel and other non-toxic shot. Lately, Patternmaster has developed their "Superchoke," which is reported to handle smaller shot sizes than their "Standard" models. The Patternmaster tubes work on the principle of wad retardation, quickly separating the wad and shot cup from the payload, rather than muzzle constriction. Several years ago, competitive trap shooters experimented with straight rifling to slow shot shell wads to quickly separate them from the shot payload. Hasting's straight-rifled shotgun barrels work on a similar principle of wad retardation.

Pure Gold–This newcomer to the choke tube business has made some serious inroads into the turkey tube business. Solid patterns from most of the guns I've tested promise to lead this firearms accessory company into a leadership position in the industry.

Remington Arms Co.–Big Green's chokes are the most consistent factory-supplied turkey tubes. The .660 and .665 diameter 12 gauge tubes are sure to work with a wide range of turkey loads. It's ironic to note that non-Remington turkey loads have pattered better than most of this company's own turkey loads.

Rhino–One of the most devastating guns I've shot is a Mossberg 835 Ulti-Mag owned by a good friend, Jason Morrow, one of the NWTF's television field producers. It is fitted with a Rhino choke, and consistently prints very dense patterns with Winchester Hi-Velocity No. 4 shot.

Strangler–Another new choke has been designed by Strangler of Winfield,

Choke Manufacturer	Phone	Website/email
Ballistic Specialties Inc.	800-276-2550	www.angleport.com
Briley	785-632-3169	email-hastings@kansas.net
Browning	801-876-2711	www.bronwing.com
Carlson's	785-626-3700	www.carlsonschokes.com
Colonial	800-949-8088	www.colonialarms.com
Comp-N-Choke	888-875-7906	www.comp-n-choke.com
Gobblin' Thunder	888-875-7906	www.comp-n-choke.com
Hastings	785-632-3169	email-hastings@kansas.net
H.S. Strut Under Taker	319-395-0321	www.hunterspec.com
Lohman Long Shot	800-922-9034	www.outlandsports.com
M.A.D. Mad Max	800-922-9034	www.outlandsports.com
Mossberg	800-989-4867	www.mossberg.com
Nu-Line Guns	636-447-4501	www.nulineguns.com
Patternmaster	608-623-3131	talktous@patternmaster.com
Pure Gold	803-328-6829	N/A
Remington Arms Co.	800-243-9700	www.remingtonarms.com
Rhino	352-528-6110	N/A
Strangler	318-628-4114	N/A
Tru-Glo-Truchoke	972-77-0300	www.truglosights.com

Innovation Leads to New Barrel Design

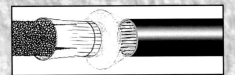

Hastings' straight-rifled barrel keeps the plastic wad from spinning, which reduces shot dipersion.

As the seasons pass, new innovations in turkey guns and loads seem to keep popping up like mushrooms after a spring rain. One twist in shotgun barrels, or rather the lack thereof, is straight rifling, introduced in 1995 by Hastings.

Shotgun wads and shot columns spin as they travel down a smooth shotgun barrel. Although a precise amount of spin helps stabilize a bullet or arrow, this characteristic has a negative impact when trying to achieve tight, even shot patterns.

Not long after Hastings introduced their new barrels, I got a telephone call from fellow outdoors writer Brook Elliott telling me about the new design. The way it's described, the barrel's straight (rather than twisted) lands and grooves are reported to retard or prevent wad rotation as it travels down the barrel. It's reasonable to think that a shot column that isn't rotating is less likely to spin off stray pellets due to centrifugal force. Having a few pellets moving in any direction other than straight at the intended target will cause a chain reaction that will continue to multiply as they bump into other pellets. Reducing this tendency should create tighter patterns.

Several trips to the range showed me that the Hastings concept holds some promise. Although I didn't reach those hard-to-obtain 90 percent patterns at 40 yards, I was pleasantly surprised by its performance with selected loads.

The acid test for any hunting gun is how it performs on game. I was able to shoot three longbeards with a Remington 870 fitted with the Hastings barrel that spring. The third bird taken was a South Carolina Eastern turkey that I had located on game management land in a well-hunted area late in the season. I found the two-year-old tom strutting on a power line right-of-way on private ground within calling distance of the public hunting area. After almost an hour of calling, the longbeard finally decided to cross a dirt road that marked the boundary of the game management land. A few minutes later, the bird had closed the gap to 38 yards when a hen started yelping from the direction he had come. I gave a sharp cluck from a Knight & Hale diaphragm, to pull the tom out of strut, and lit the fire behind a 2¼ ounce load of Nitro No. 6s. The show was over. While admiring the bird, I closely examined the effects of the shot. The swarm of No. 6 shot was devastating.

At the range I patterned 12 different loads through the 12-gauge Hastings barrel. The 24-inch barrel was fitted with a Hastings choke tube that measured .655 at the muzzle. In addition to calculating the averages for pellets in a 30-inch circle at 40 yards, I also measured the number of hits within the vital area drawn on the Winchester patterning targets. Going one step further, I sought a more refined method of measurement by counting the number of pellets within a 10-inch circle at 40 yards, and averaged that as well (see the results in the accompanying chart).

The top-performing load was the Nitro 3-inch magnum loaded with 2¼ ounces of No. 6 shot. This load averaged 81.7 percent within a 30-inch circle at 40 yards. These Nitro loads are hot! I experienced sticky extraction with several shots, telling me that the load was producing pressure near the maximum tolerance for the Remington action.

Federal's top performer was a 3-inch, 2-ounce load of No. 4s. It averaged 16 pellets in the vitals, 72 hits within a 10-inch circle and 86 percent within a 30-inch circle. Remington's 2-ounce load of No. 5s performed well. Winchester's two best performers came from a 1⅞-ounce load of No. 2s and a 1½-ounce load of No. 5s in a 2¾-inch shell.

An attractive feature of the Hastings barrel is the adjustable sights. After testing various loads, it was apparent that different loads had slightly different points of impact. Fine-tuning the sights with a particular load is critical, especially when shooting at close range.

Ammo	Shot size	Load weight	% 30-inch circle	Hits in vitals	Pellets / 10" circle
Federal	4	2	86.0	16	72
Federal	5	2	75.3	16	66
Federal	7½	2	75.0	22	130
Winchester	2	1⅞	80.8	14	39
Winchester	4	2	61.1	7	55
Winchester	5	1½	82.5	6	42
Winchester	6	2	63.6	9	55
Remington	4	2	70.0	5	45
Remington	5	2	76.2	20	66
Nitro	5	2¼	58.7	24	62
Nitro*	6	2¼	81.7	31	121
Nitro*	5 x 7½	2¼	68.1	29	88

* Sticky Extraction

Louisiana. Working on similar principles of quick wad-and-shot separation, Strangler tubes have proven themselves to be strong performers with non-toxic shot in waterfowling applications. Early reports from shooting writers whom have tested the Strangler tubes indicate that these tubes perform well with tungsten turkey loads and various lead loads as well.

In response to one of my columns in the *Turkey Call* magazine, hunter Ken Szymanski wrote:

I recently purchased a Mossberg 9200 12 gauge. After patterning the gun with Mossberg's X-full Accu-choke, I feel that I would be better off with an after-market extended turkey choke.

Can you make any suggestions as to what choke tubes work well in this gun. I like to shoot Winchester XX 2-oz. loads of No. 5s in the spring and Federal 2-oz. loads of No. 4s in the fall from my Remington 870. These loads have shown some promise in the Mossberg. Are the new ported chokes better than the solid type? What about straight rifling choke tubes? Are the ported tubes that much louder and do they really reduce recoil significantly?

Ken Szymanski
Ford City, Pennsylvania

I replied. The choke tubes that have worked the best in one of the Mossberg 9200s that I have shot are the Carlson's .665 and the Comp-N-Choke .665. These tubes printed tight, even patterns with Winchester Supreme 2-ounce loads of No. 4, 5 or 6 shot. I've also had good success with the Winchester 1¾-ounce high velocity loads of No. 5s.

The effective difference between ported, non-ported or straight-rifled choke tubes really depends on the gun. The wise practice of testing various loads and shot sizes in a particular gun is equally important to trying different choke tubes. The principle of straight rifling in choke tubes, or barrels for that matter, has been proven to even out shot patterns. Stopping the shot cup from rotating after leaving the barrel keeps the shot column from spinning. Centrifugal force will cause patterns to open up rather than stay tight and uniform.

The noise problem associated with porting to reduce recoil is not typically applicable to shotgun choke tubes. Centerfire rifle and pistol porting incorporates ports that are aimed back at the shooter, which pulls the firearm forward at the same time recoil is being exerted backward. The combination of the two forces helps reduce recoil at the shoulder and reduces muzzle rise. Shotgun choke tubes are ported to bleed off the gas cloud following the shot column to improve pattern performance. The cuts or holes in choke tubes are normally straight or aimed forward, which do nothing for recoil and shouldn't increase muzzle blast.

The bottom line is to try various choke sizes to get your best performer. Put in the extra effort and you'll up your confidence level for making a clean, ethical shot on that old longbeard this season.

Barrel porting

Clay target shooters were the first shotgunners to benefit from porting their shotgun barrels to help reduce felt recoil. Holes drilled on the top of the barrel near the muzzle vent off gas, which retards muzzle rise. When the escaping gas pushes back down on the barrel–similar in principle to a jet engine propelling an airplane –it keeps the gun stock from raising into the shooter's face and rearward into the shoulder. Since the gun is directing its recoil more into the shoulder, where it is intended, instead of the face, felt recoil tends to be less. One drawback to shooting a ported gun is the increase in muzzle blast. For shotgun porting to reduce actual recoil, the ports would need to be directed to the rear toward the shooter, which would be damaging to shooters without hearing protection. A perfect example can be borrowed from the recoil reducer incorporated into Browning's Ballistic Optimizing Shooting System (B.O.S.S.). The B.O.S.S. does a good job cutting recoil, but Browning has stopped selling their rifles with the recoil reducer as standard equipment. Hunters shooting the B.O.S.S. with the recoil reducer in place while hunting were experiencing hearing damage and lawsuits followed.

Against the Wind
Longer vs. shorter barrels—
does length make a difference in turkey gun performance?

Four camo-clad turkey hunters walked along single-file, the leader scanning the South Dakota Black Hills ahead for a Merriam's gobbler. Hunting by sight was about the only option available, owing to the howling winds.

South Dakota outfitter John Hauer, writer Roger Hook, Hunter's Specialties' Steve Puppe and I were trying to roost a gobbler or two for the next morning's hunt. With the wind constantly blowing 20 mph, with frequent gusts reaching 35 mph, our little hunting party spoke often of the difficulties faced when hunting in high winds. Hearing a tom gobble more than a few yards downwind was nearly impossible.

Although somewhat less of a concern than not being able to hear birds, I wondered what kind of tricks the wind might play on a 12-gauge turkey load in conditions as extreme as these. I learned years ago while shooting in long-range rifle competition that the faster a bullet travels and the more it weighs, the better. Some basic laws of physics dictate that the slower an object travels, the more it is pushed around by other forces, such as wind.

Several times I have wondered if short-barreled turkey guns were giving up much velocity when compared with longer barrels.

Conversations with ballistics experts at different ammunition companies revealed that shotshell velocities published in catalogs were derived from shooting turkey loads from 30-inch test barrels—a far cry longer than most turkey gun barrels sold today. How much slower these turkey loads traveled was a question I had to solve, so I decided to do a little testing.

I picked six turkey loads to shoot through a Mossberg 9200 semi-automatic 12 gauge. For comparison, I took a 28-inch barrel and fired five rounds of each load through a .660 extra-full turkey choke across an Oehler chronograph, to get average velocities. Next, I shot the same five-round battery without a choke tube installed. To get a good range of comparison, I cut the barrel off in 2-inch increments to 26, 24, and 22 inches. The table on the following page shows the results of the testing. Predictably, longer barrels shot faster than shorter barrel lengths. A surprising result of the test was the significant difference a tight turkey choke makes on velocities 3 feet from the barrel. The velocities ranged from 60 feet per second (fps) to 94 fps between the .660 constriction and velocities from a cylinder bore. It's the same effect as putting a smaller nozzle on a garden hose: the smaller the nozzle, the higher the pressure.

One of the reasons to be concerned about the velocity of your turkey loads is whether or not they

FORMER NWTF field producer Bob Thompson filmed the author bagging this South Dakota tom. We learned that larger shot sizes are less affected by windy conditions.

VELOCITY & BARREL LENGTH

Manufacturer	Load	Barrel Length	Avg. Velocity fps. @ 3 ft.
WW	1¾ oz. No. 5	22	1,228
WW	1¾ oz. No. 5	24	1,227
WW	1¾ oz. No. 5	26	1,266
WW	1¾ oz. No. 5	28	1,292
WW	1¾ oz. No. 5	28*	1,352
WW	1¾ oz. No. 5	30**	1,300
WW	2 oz. No. 5	22	1,124
WW	2 oz. No. 5	24	1,124
WW	2 oz. No. 5	26	1,129
WW	2 oz. No. 5	28	1,147
WW	2 oz. No. 5	28*	1,220
WW	2 oz. No. 5	30**	1,125
Federal	1¾ oz. No. 4	22	1,251
Federal	1¾ oz. No. 4	24	1,240
Federal	1¾ oz. No. 4	26	1,269
Federal	1¾ oz. No. 4	28	1,288
Federal	1¾ oz. No. 4	28*	1,340
Federal	1¾ oz. No. 4	30**	1,300
Federal	2 oz. No. 4	22	1,069
Federal	2 oz. No. 4	24	1,094
Federal	2 oz. No. 4	26	1,103
Federal	2 oz. No. 4	28	1,124
Federal	2 oz. No. 4	28*	1,173
Federal	2 oz. No. 4	30**	1,175
Remington	2 oz. No. 4	22	1,040
Remington	2 oz. No. 4	24	1,068
Remington	2 oz. No. 4	26	1,059
Remington	2 oz. No. 4	28	1,078
Remington	2 oz. No. 4	28*	1,172
Remington	2 oz. No. 4	30**	1,175
Kent	1⅝ oz. No. 5	22	1,213
Kent	1⅝ oz. No. 5	24	1,226
Kent	1⅝ oz. No. 5	26	1,257
Kent	1⅝ oz. No. 5	28	1,273
Kent	1⅝ oz. No. 5	28*	1,366
Kent	1⅝ oz. No. 5	30**	1,330

* Barrel with .660 constriction turkey choke installed.
** Manufacturer's published velocity, typically fired from a 30-inch test barrel.

still have the punch down-range to cleanly dispatch the intended quarry. Although minor, another factor is how much the core of the pattern drops or how far wind drift will change your gun's point of impact. For instance, a 2-ounce load of No. 6 shot that starts out at 1,125 fps will drop over three inches at 40 yards. The same load will be blown off center 6 inches in a 10 mph wind at the same distance.

I got another surprise from the testing. The range of velocities between shots for a particular load in the same barrel sometimes had wide varia-

continued on next page

tions. The high-to-low spread for loads shot from a cylinder bore was about 13 fps, while shots from a barrel with a .660 choke tube installed had a spread that was about 40 fps. The Remington loads had the greatest spread from shot to shot at 68 fps. Winchester's 2-ounce loads of No. 5 shot had a 15 fps range with choke tube installed, and the Kent loads posted a minuscule range of 4 fps. Boiling this down, with greater velocity spreads, less-consistent patterns will result.

Keep in mind that velocity readings are 2 percent to 5 percent higher than results from factory testing equipment. Velocities also may be slightly higher due to temperatures in the mid-90s during testing.

My conclusions from the testing lead me to believe that factory turkey load velocities are pretty close to what you will find when shooting a 22-inch-barrel turkey gun. When any turkey load crosses the 40-yard mark, it is only traveling slightly more than half the speed it had at the muzzle. So, starting out faster via a longer barrel will give a slight increase in energy and penetration when pellets strike home. When trying to cleanly kill a big, tough bird, you may wish to consider the trade-off between an easier-to-carry short barrel or a longer barrel that will raise velocities and increase effective range by about 5 yards.

When hunting in windy conditions and your turkey gun patterns equally well with different shot sizes, pick the larger size, to reduce the effect wind plays. When faced with high-wind conditions, picking shots closer than your normal maximum effective range would be an ethical choice as well.

IN TURKEY HUNTING applications, little, if anything, is gained by shooting a gun with a ported barrel.

Back boring

Back boring a shotgun barrel is achieved by cutting the inside diameter between the forcing cone and the muzzle. A 12-gauge that is back bored is essentially a 10-gauge gun with a 12-gauge chamber. The benefit of back boring is that pressure is lower, which is less disruptive to shot columns. The drop in pressure also reduces recoil. When shooting the heavy 3½-inch 12-gauge loads back boring really shines. As mentioned previously, the Mossberg 835 and Browning Invector Plus barrels are back bored.

Competent gunsmiths can also back bore shotguns if the barrel thickness is ample enough to allow the process and leave the gun safe to shoot.

Elongating forcing cones

The forcing cone is the angled step between the chamber and the barrel. It serves as a "ramp" to guide the shot charge from the larger area of the chamber and the barrel. Most factory shotguns have forcing cones that are rather short and abrupt. Extending the length of the forcing cone is easier on shot as it makes the transition to the barrel. Lengthening a forcing cone will also reduce chamber pressure and recoil. One drawback to lengthening a forcing cone is that it will not always

improve pattern performance. Before you have your gunsmith start reaming out the barrel of your favorite turkey gun, be sure to try a wide range of turkey loads and choke tubes.

Sleeving barrels

Another approach to barrel modification is to have a gunsmith "sleeve" your turkey gun. Short sleeves are 3 to 4 inches in length, with longer options available. The barrel's internal diameter is reamed out to allow a sleeve to be swaged or soldered in place. The concept behind sleeving a barrel is to make the transition from the bore more gradual than found in a standard choke. Sleeving works much like a longer forcing cone. Although most practiced gunsmiths can sleeve a barrel to your specifications, working with a specialist in turkey guns like Mark Bansner from Allentown, Pennsylvania, might be a good idea.

14. *Behind the Chamber*

If you've covered the basic tune-ups available for squeezing the most performance from your scattergun's barrel, try some of these ideas to create the ultimate turkey gun.

Custom Triggers

Shooters know the value of a crisp trigger pull, to squeeze out the last shred of rifle accuracy. Fear of a lawsuit forces most firearms manufacturers to build their guns with heavy, sloppy trigger pulls. Although it does not make as much difference in turkey hunting applications, it does have an effect on how accurately you can shoot a tight-patterning turkey gun. A qualified gunsmith can improve your turkey gun's performance by adjusting its trigger pull. Tuning sear engagement, reworking springs, removing trigger over-travel and reducing trigger pull weight are the primary jobs a gunsmith can perform.

CUSTOM TUNE-UPS can increase the range and effectiveness of your favorite turkey gun.

HASTINGS manufactured a high-grade trigger group for the Remington 870. The after-market trigger gives an 870 a crisp, rifle-like trigger pull.

Another way to improve your gun's trigger is to replace it with a complete after-market trigger assembly. Several years ago, Hastings offered a replacement trigger group for the Remington Model 870. I added this well-tuned trigger assembly to my first turkey gun, and noticed an immediate improvement in feel and performance. This Model 870 also doubles as a deer gun. When I switch to a rifled barrel and shoot slugs, the improved trigger pull is an obvious advantage.

Stocks—Wood vs. Synthetic

Synthetic stocks were slow to catch on, but as more gun writers learned of their advantages and wrote positive articles about them, America's shooters followed suit by switching beautiful wood stocks for space-age handles. After-market plastic stock makers sprouted like mushrooms after a warm spring rain. These stocks were made of materials such as fiberglass, Kevlar or other injection-molded plastics. The obvious advantage of a plastic stock is its imperviousness to whatever Mother Nature can dredge up.

Wood stocks swell, split, crack and warp when subjected to wet weather. A plastic stock just takes it in stride.

When firearms manufacturers decided plastic stocks were more than a passing fad, many re-tooled to add synthetics to their product lines. Add a coat of your favorite camouflage, and you've got an attractive, hardworking tool that's ready to tackle any weather condition.

Today, the metal parts of your turkey gun are still vulnerable to rusting if subjected to wet conditions. Glock handguns became famous for their plastic frames and slides, which create rugged, ready-for-anything shooting systems. Benelli USA was the first sporting arms manufacturer to offer a "plastic" shotgun, the Nova. This newcomer incorporates a one-piece stock and receiver with metallic inserts to give the action the needed strength to handle both light and heavy 3½-inch magnum 12-gauge loads equally well.

Another stock design made possible by the advance from

wood to synthetics is the tactical pistol-grip. Standard stocks force your hand and wrist into an uncomfortable bind when shouldering a rifle or shotgun. A vertical, tactical-type pistol grip allows you to keep a gun shouldered for a long period in comfort. These new-style grips also help better absorb felt recoil, which is a major consideration when shooting sledge-hammer turkey loads.

Eager to produce innovative, practical designs, Benelli USA has introduced two straight pistol-grip turkey guns built on the highly popular Super Black Eagle and the M-1 Field. Their early acceptance by well-known gun experts will probably usher in a new wave in turkey gun design.

In principle, thumb-hole stocks work similarly to straight pistol-grip stocks, increasing the grip angle to more comfortable dimensions. During the early 1990s, I discussed with different gun manufacturing representatives and stock makers the theoretical usefulness of thumb-hole or straight pistol-grip stocks for turkey guns. I also shared my futuristic ideas with top management at the National Wild Turkey Federation, but it fell on deaf ears.

When Benelli launched their new pistol-grip turkey guns in April 2002 at a writers' seminar, I got a glimpse of the future in turkey guns. The turkey hunt was a success, with several writers bagging longbeards with the newly designed guns. What I witnessed the last day of the event, as we packed our bags to return home, really got my attention. An experienced turkey hunter arrived at the outfitter's lodge ready to begin his hunt after our crew cleared out of camp. We began chatting, and I explained that the purpose of the hunt was to trial the new stock design. He smiled, walked outside, and returned a minute later with his own cased turkey gun. To my surprise, he pulled out a 12-gauge Super Black Eagle with a straight-grip Benelli tactical stock. He had his hometown gun shop order an extra tactical stock and switch it out.

My fondness for more ergonomic turkey gun stocks rose a notch when I tried out a prototype Mossberg design that incorporated a Speed Feed stock and a factory Mossy Oak camo finish.

Stock Options

After a day and a half trying to double-team a particular Arkansas tom we had nicknamed "Old Long-gobble," Roger Hook and I advanced up the spine of a ridge to get closer to the bird's strut zone. Listening to the distinctively-voiced bird advance and retreat along the ridgetop gave me audible clues as to what this bird was doing.

The time felt right when Old Long-gobble strutted to the farthest end of his strut zone, so I scrambled a hundred yards up the trail along the ridge to the edge of a little clearing to set up. Fearing that I might have bumped the bird,

BENELLI'S NEW SteadyGrip™ stock helps reduce felt recoil and raises gun maneuverability.

I clucked once to check his progress. Not getting the answer I wanted, I waited a few moments and cutt hard at the bird with a mouth call. He obliged me with his unique invitation to join him for a woodland tryst. Over the next 45 minutes we traded calls as the bird advanced toward my setup. Since I was set up in a relatively open spot and the bird stubbornly held his ground just out of sight over a rise 35 yards away, I stayed frozen in shooting position for a long time. When my right leg went to sleep from the somewhat awkward sitting position I chose, I just ignored it. Tensed from the excitement, my right arm started going numb, but I couldn't ignore that. Every two or three minutes I relaxed my grip on the stock to slowly flex my hand and wrist, while the bird shook the ground with his gobbles from just over the rise.

I was relieved when I heard Roger strike up his Cody slate call down the trail behind me. I quit calling, hoping the bird would move forward to check out Roger's calls. Seconds ticked into minutes as the tom strutted and drummed just out of sight. When he gobbled close and to the left, I slowly swung the gun toward the sound. Stepping past a stunted cedar bush at 21 yards, Old Long-gobble lived up to his nickname one last time.

This hunt played out like many others with regard to my trigger hand—not to mention

A THUMB HOLE STOCK gives the shooter more control when shooting from odd positions.

several other parts of my anatomy—becoming numb after long periods locked in the ready position. Experience with thumb-hole rifle stocks led me to believe that applying the same design to a shotgun stock would lead to a more relaxed and comfortable grip.

Several years ago, I searched for a thumb-hole stock for my Remington 870, to get a more comfortable grip on the situation. I had several conversations with a fiberglass stock maker about this issue, but the outcome was that it was too expensive for the company to tool up a new mold for a stock that had questionable sales potential. I located another stock maker that offered walnut thumb-hole versions that would fit a shotgun. When I learned that the price of the walnut stock surpassed the cost of a new gun, I decided to shelve the project.

I didn't think much about this subject until a conversation in 1998 with Mossberg's Matt Wettish. He had fitted a

camouflaged pistol-grip stock to his Model 835 Ulti-Mag 12 gauge, and was happy with the setup. I was pleasantly surprised a few days later when a pistol-grip stock fitted for a Model 9200 showed up at my door.

Since then, I've replaced the original stock on the 9200 with the radical-looking handle. I took the outfit on a late-season hunt in New York and was pleased with the fit. In hunting situations the pistol-grip stock does its intended job of keeping the trigger hand and wrist in line with the rest of the arm, thus creating a more relaxed grip.

Passing the pistol-grip-fitted shotgun among turkey hunters has met with mixed reviews. Some don't like the looks of the stock, saying it looks a little too militaristic for their tastes. Other comments have centered around the usefulness of a pistol-grip stock on a gun with a top-tang safety.

There's no denying that today's camouflaged, short-

the addition of camo in various forms.

To improve handling in tight quarters, such as blinds and in thick cover, turkey guns have borrowed the shorter barrels seen for decades on riot guns. The short barrels make law enforcement shotguns easy to handle in tight quarters, such as a patrol car. Likewise, bobbed barrels on turkey guns facilitate handling ease while carrying slung over the shoulder or while in a seated shooting position.

One turkey gun development slow to be accepted is the addition of a pistol grip or thumb-hole butt stock. What these stocks offer is a comfortable grip that imparts less strain on the hunter's trigger hand and wrist. After several minutes gripping a conventional stock while waiting for an approaching gobbler, I often experience pain from my shoulder down through my wrist. The primary cause is tensed muscles kept frozen in the same position for an extended period. Something that helps ease the tension in my shooting arm is to relax and straighten the angle of my wrist by releasing the grip and slowly moving my hand to ease the tension. Since movement is the best way to be caught by a vigilant gobbler looking for your calling position, this isn't always practical. The use of a pistol-grip stock is much more relaxing when trying to be as still as possible.

Previously, a small handful of custom stock makers have offered thumb-hole stocks for shotguns, but these stocks were expensive and hard to find.

In 1998, Mossberg built a limited number of camouflaged pistol-grip stocks for their Model 835 Ulti-Mag and 9200 12-gauge turkey guns for trial use. I got a new stock for my 9200 late during the spring season and was able to carry it afield for several hunts. The only drawback of the pistol-grip stock on the Mossberg shotguns is the placement of the top tang safety. The safety isn't within reach of the thumb on the trigger hand while gripping the stock.

barreled turkey guns fitted with rifle sights or scopes, slings, ultra-tight choke tubes, etc., have come a long way from the fowling pieces of 30 years ago. Only time and market demand will tell if new styling in shotgun stocks will be the next wave in turkey gun technology.

It seems that today's turkey guns have achieved a plateau of performance that makes them consistent tools for taking birds at 40 yards. Several of the changes in styling have transformed a wing shooter's fowling piece into a rifle-like shotgun with refinements geared toward the specialized needs of turkey hunters.

Since the objective of a shot at a wild turkey is to put several pellets into the vital head and neck areas, the addition of rifle sights or scopes has answered the need. The necessity of hiding turkey guns from keen-eyed birds resulted in

15. Turkey Guns Get a New Look

"Camouflaged tapes have been used with a lot of success to mask a gun's shiny surfaces."

Over the last 25 years, firearms manufacturers have refined their shotguns to appeal to several different groups of shooters. Prior to the 1970s, major gunmakers divided their shotgun lines between clay bird shooters, law enforcement and hunters. The clays shooters were primarily focused on trap and skeet, while the law enforcement crowd required short-barreled, high-capacity weapons that were utterly reliable. Hunters, as a group, primarily sought scatterguns that were versatile enough to bag upland and small game, waterfowl and the occasional Whitetail. Hunting guns came from the factory with fixed chokes, blued metal and glossy finishes on their stocks.

Today, hunting shotguns have evolved to fit the specific needs of hunters pursuing specific game animals. Turkey hunting is one of the best examples. Gun makers listened when experienced turkey hunters asked for shorter barrels, tighter chokes and finishes that blended with the colors found in the woods.

Prior to these relatively new advances in turkey guns, many turkey hunters hid the shiny finishes of their scatterguns from a gobbler's keen eyesight with either drab, dull spray paint, or they masked barrels and stocks with camouflage-patterned tape.

The paint or tape method still works as well

POPULAR CAMOUFLAGE designs allow the turkey hunter many options.

**BENELLI NOVA "SB"
ADVANTAGE TIMBER H. D.**

**BENELLI M1
ADVANTAGE TIMBER H.D.**

today as it did years ago, but new products and advances in technology give a hunter more ways to hide his shotgun from a tom's prying eyes. One such product that's caught on with turkey and deer hunters is Gun Chaps, made by Kane Products. These zippered cloth-and-vinyl covers come in different camouflage patterns and are custom-made in either a one- or two-piece construction to fit the dimensions of over 100 shotguns and rifles. Kane also makes Barrel Chaps, a relatively new product in their line of gun covers. This device is made to fit either single- or double-barreled shotguns and rifles. It's simply a sleeve that slides over the barrel. Gun Chaps are offered in woodland and Realtree camo patterns.

Another product that's been used successfully to camouflage shotguns is a stretchy, gauze-like material made by Expand-O-Flage. It was a one-size-fits-all tube of camo material that had to be cut to fit a particular weapon. Tape was used to hold it in place.

Expand-O-Flage is no longer in business, but a close facsimile can be made by using an NWTF Sack-Up gun sock and trimming and taping it to fit a particular gun.

Camouflaged tapes have been used with a lot of success to mask a gun's shiny surfaces. The first turkey hunter I ever met, a friend's uncle in north Georgia, covered his trusty long-barreled pump 12 gauge with white cloth athletic tape, and used green and black permanent felt-tipped markers to color the tape. A sizable collection of turkey beards hanging

in his gun cabinet gave mute testimony that he was on the right track. In the years since, a host of companies have come out with camo tapes in every pattern you can imagine. Most tapes have an adhesive backing, while others are held in place by their stretchy, elastic nature.

Several companies have offered spray-on camo paints that were either permanent or semi- permanent. The semi-permanent paints could be peeled off, and were more of a skin than real paint. With either type paint, two or three

EXPAND-O-FLAGE and Gun Chaps (right) are camo options.

CAMOUFLAGE tape is a good temporary fix for hiding a shiny finish.

colors are needed to complete the job. After masking off surfaces that shouldn't be painted, such as slides on pump shotguns, or critical action parts, a base coat of a dull dark green or brown is applied to the entire gun. Then a contrasting lighter color is used to break up the gun's outline. Take several small leaves and lay them randomly on the gun, then spray on the lighter color to create the outline of the leaves on the stock and barrel. Bohning archery products sells both a waterproof camo tape and permanent camo spray paints that I've used to camouflage bows, guns and other sporting equipment.

The newest craze in gun camo is the factory-applied finish that replicates some of the major camouflage patterns on the market. This process is actually a film that the guns are dipped in that quickly dries to a tough, permanent finish. The NWTF 1992 Gun of the Year, a Remington 11-87, was adorned in Trebark using this process. The NWTF youth guns made by New England Firearms for the past three years also used this process to apply a Mossy Oak pattern. Several other rifles and shotguns are offered with this process, in the aforementioned patterns as well as Realtree, but buying a new gun is the only way to get your hands on one at this time.

Depending on which direction you take, either a new factory-camouflaged model or dressing up your favorite turkey gun, making your fowling piece less conspicuous will up your chances for success.

16. *Seeing is Believing*

What if your shotgun doesn't center the pattern where you're aiming? One option is to have the barrel bent by a competent gunsmith so that it shoots where it is aimed. On the other hand, adjustable rifle-type sights can get you on target with little fuss and expense.

Several models available clamp onto your shotgun barrel rib, or you can have a gunsmith install a set. Many of the fiber-optic sights offered today work well, but are rather fragile under field conditions. I have no doubt that I am not the only turkey hunter who has had these sights get bumped off and missed shots at turkeys. Some shotgun manufacturers have actually gone back to installing plain bead sights on their turkey guns to counter complaints of weak fiber-optic sights.

A PENTTAX Lightseeker SG Plus scope is one of the author's favorites.

AIMTECH saddle mounts accept Weaver-type scope rings.

Whether you go with an after-market addition or factory sights, it's a simple matter to do some fine tuning to get everything lined up.

In the cross hairs

Another option is a low-powered scope. A zero-to-3X magnification will work the best. Some scopes have standard cross hairs, while others offer various rangefinding reticles. Either diamond-shaped or circular, the center of the reticle covers a specified area, which corresponds to different measurements at different ranges. With practice, you can gauge the range to a gobbler by comparing the reticle's center area to a part of the bird's body, such as the distance from the top of his head to his beard. Pentax, Bushnell, Leupold and Burris scopes have proven top performers on my turkey guns over the years. Pentax probably took the most aggressive approach to the turkey-hunting market when they released their 0X-4X variable Lightseeker SG Plus. This scope was created with still-target competition and actual hunting situations in mind. Whichever scope you chose, make sure that the eye relief is long enough to keep your face away from the rear of the scope. Although I've been lucky, I have seen a few turkey hunters who got too close to their scopes and got some nasty cuts when the scopes came back in recoil.

I recall the best example of how short eye-relief scopes and turkey loads don't mix. *Turkey Call* television field producer Jason Morrow and I were tasked with prepping guns for guests who would be hunting with the *Turkey Call* television camera crew. I mounted a Simmons low-power variable turkey scope on Jason's 835 Mossberg. The first shots with dove loads for short-range sighters posed no problems. I told Jason that I felt that the scope did not have enough eye relief for firing heavy loads, but he shrugged it off as he chambered a 3½-inch High-Velocity Winchester turkey load. When he pulled the trigger the result was sad, but predictable. He still has a crescent-shaped scar across the bridge of his nose.

Over the past few seasons, I've had success with "dot" scopes. I've had equal success with Simmons, Aimpoint and Burris models. It's simple to adjust the cross hairs or dot to cover the center of your shot pattern. It's also easier to keep your gun on target, even in odd positions. A big advantage is that your sights and your target are in perfect focus at the same time.

Once you get accustomed to shooting with a scope or rifle sights you'll learn what I have: Getting lined up on a cagey old gobbler is every bit as fast as shooting with standard bead sights. So when opening day rolls around, make sure all of your equipment, especially your turkey gun, is ready to go hunting.

A Closer Look at Scopes for Turkey Guns

Like many turkey hunters, I had a preseason spring ritual that was nearly as enjoyable as going afield with a gun in hand. During the ten seasons I lived in rural South Carolina, I rose early most March days to greet the morning standing along some backwoods dirt road listening for gobblers. More often than not, I heard nothing but crows and cardinals, but when I did raise a gobbler, it was a singular thrill.

On one occasion, I stopped atop a red clay hill to call into the creek valley that snaked through my deer hunting club. I blew a crow call first, to see if there was an "easy" bird that would shock-gobble at my avian insults. When I got no reply, I switched to a favorite box call and ripped off a short series of yelps and cutts. Before the call's echo died, I heard an old bird gobble back. He was 500 yards away, and proba-bly standing on an old wooden logging bridge. I had run a gobbler off the bridge in mid-January when I drove in to retrieve my deer stands. One thing for sure, he liked hanging around that old bridge. I called him "The Troll."

When he gobbled a second time, it was evident that he was getting closer, so I packed up and drove out the way I came in. When I got to the other side of the 200-acre clear-cut, I stopped again to call down a different creek drain, to try locating another bird. The next time I hit a lick on that box call, the same gobbler answered again. He was still a thousand yards away, but he had marched down the road 250 yards and was starting up the hill to meet me.

A tom that willing to come to a call three days before season begged for an encounter come opening morning. A few days prior to my encounter with that longbeard, I had received a package from Pentax containing their new 0X-4X Lightseeker SG Plus scope. The Pentax folks in Englewood, Colorado, were paying attention when they came to market with this scope. Crisp optics weren't the only brag features on this scope. The product development staff had been following the National Wild Turkey Federation's still-target shooting matches, and wanted to make a scope that would serve

REMINGTON'S CANTILEVER Scope bases attach to barrel rather than the receiver.

double-duty in competition and in the hunting field. This scope's cross hairs centered on a small circular reticle that matched up well with the scoring ring on the NWTF's official competition targets. I mounted the scope with Weaver rings and an Aimtech mount on a well-worn Remington 11-87, and was anxious to put it to use. When I met up with The Troll, I knew that the fun was about to begin.

An hour before first light, I gathered my vest and gun, and began the quarter-mile walk down the red clay road toward The Troll's creek-side haunt. As I walked, I dropped a high-velocity load of Winchester No. 5s into the open action and eased the bolt shut, then thumbed four more into the magazine.

I eased across the bridge and continued climbing up the road until it flattened out. I reached an opening planted in winter wheat, and decided to make my stand. I walked to a likely spot and planted a decoy in the center of the road. Picking out a suitable pine, I got into position and waited for the morning to begin. Erring on the side of caution, I kept my calls quiet and waited for the gobbler to make the first calls of the morning. When there was good shooting light, I grew impatient and raised a crow call to get things started. My sixth sense told me to hold off, so I traded the call for my trusty box call and gently stroked three soft yelps. The

gobbler nearly blew my hat off. He was roosted 30 yards to my left, just off the clearing. He began strutting on the limb and I could plainly hear his wings dragging on the bark. I guess he had seen me walking through the dark opening nearly an hour before, and decided to keep his mouth shut until I made my first calls. He gobbled several more times as I inched my gun to the left to cover a likely landing spot on the edge of the clearing.

Cheek tight to the stock, I yelped a couple of notes on a mouth call and waited for him to fly down. I'll never forget hearing his wingbeats while I peered through the Pentax scope. I had both eyes open, and caught his dark form sailing down to land squarely in

the cross hairs. For reasons I can't explain, I held fire and watched the gobbler march straight to the decoy to check out his new girlfriend. I repositioned the Remington, and found his noggin in the cross hairs once again. A sharp cutt on a mouth call and he stood on his tiptoes to find me, as I took the slack out of the trigger. Needless to say, I was pleased with my opening day success and the performance of the scoped Remington.

Reasons for using a scope

Previously, I touched on the use of scopes on turkey guns as a sight option. The biggest reason that I think turkey hunters should consider scopes is poor vision. A recent demographics survey conducted by the NWTF revealed that the median age of male turkey hunting members is 46. It's also a fact that at least 90 percent of males over age 40 need some type of vision correction. Couple weak eyesight with low light conditions prevalent in the turkey woods, and it makes getting locked on a gobbler's head a challenge. The magnification offered by a scope, and the light gathering abilities of the better-quality models, are boons for those of us who squint too much.

Vision-challenged turkey hunters also can benefit from the single focal point of a scope, in comparison to a set of open or bead sights. To properly use open sights, the sights must be kept in focus, while slightly blurring the target. You may be able to focus on the bird while you line up the sights, but in the long run, it's bet-

ter to do it the other way around. Since the dominant eye serves as the back sight for a normal shotgun setup, aligning the eye in the same position on the stock is essential to properly and consistently aiming where the gun is pointing. Improperly mounting the gun, made more difficult by adrenaline, is the biggest reason that hunters miss standing gobblers. If you don't get your face down on the stock, it's a safe bet that the shot will go high. Using a scope eliminates this malady. Essentially, you could stand on your head and shoot with a scope and hit your target, if the cross hairs are covering the right spot.

Another advantage of scope use is that, when you've got a bird in range and have him in the cross hairs or behind the dot, you can see most, or all, of the bird. Open sights only let you see what's above the barrel. This isn't a problem most of the time, but it can create problems. Reading a gobbler's body language is a talent that veteran turkey hunters exercise regularly. If a tom gets spooked while you are waiting for an open shot, and you're aiming with open sights, you may miss a subtle wing tuck that signals that he is getting nervous. A scope gives you a broader picture for gauging the gobbler's demeanor. More than once it's made the difference for me between success and failure.

A feature of many low-powered shotgun scopes is a rangefinding reticle. Although they're a poor substitute for learning how to estimate range, several of these scopes have circles, diamonds or other shapes that cover a specific area at a specific range. My personal preference lies with a small circular reticle.

Turkey hunters have a wide variety of manufacturers and models to choose from when looking for a scope. Since light-gathering qualities in a low-power scope for turkey hunting isn't as high on the priority list as, say, a rifle scope for deer hunting, some of the budget-priced models may fit the bill. No matter which end of the price spectrum you select, you will get what you pay for. Heavy-recoiling turkey loads do more than punish your shoulder; they're rough on optics. Since some of the more costly low-power models, such as Swarovski, Kahles, Zeiss, Leupold,

SADDLE MOUNTS FOR POPULAR SHOTGUNS

Shotgun Model	Ga.	Aimtech	B-Square
Benelli M1-Super 90	12	X	X
Benelli Nova	12	X	X
Benelli Super Black Eagle	12	X	
Browning Auto-5	12	X	X
Browning BPS 2¾" & 3"	12	X	X
Browning Gold 2¾" & 3"	12	X	
Browning Gold	20	X	
Ithaca 37 or 87	12	X	
Remington 1100 & 11-87*	12	X	X
Remington 1100 & 11-87	20	X	X
Remington 870, Lt.	20	X	
Remington 870	12	X	
Remington 870 3½" Mag	12	X	
Remington SP-10 Mag	10	X	
Mossberg 500 & 9200*	12	X	X
Mossberg 835	12	X	X
Winchester 1200			X
Winchester 1300	12	X	X
Winchester 1400	12	X	X
Winchester 1500	12		X

* Not listed in the Brownells catalog, but the author has mounted this model on personal guns without experiencing functioning problems.

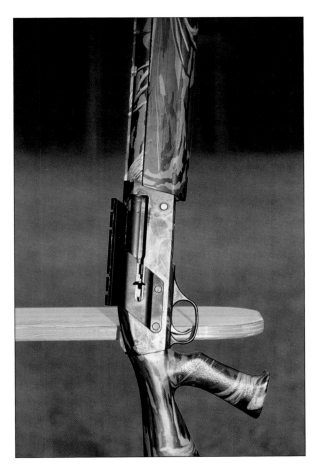

AIMTECH SADDLE mounts are a good alternative to drilling and tapping your receiver.

etc., are built to pull duty on rifles for taking dangerous game, can take excessive recoil, and will probably stand up to a lifetime of use. On the other hand, I've destroyed several of the budget-priced scopes.

Whichever model you pick, be sure that the scope has plenty of eye relief. Too little eye relief may lead to a nasty case of "scope nose." Beware of the variables with the smaller 20mm objectives. There may be enough eye relief at the lowest power settings, but at the higher magnification they tend to shrink the gap between your eye and the eyepiece.

Over the past few seasons, I've had success with "dot" scopes. I've had equal success with Simmons, Aimpoint and Burris models. The only downside to these red dot scopes is that they require batteries for operation, which have a nasty habit of running down at the worst time. Always carry a spare set of batteries when you go afield.

Mounts

Two primary types of scope-mounting systems are available. Redfield or Weaver-style rings and bases are sleek and rock-solid. Some of today's turkey guns come from the factory drilled and tapped to accept standard Redfield or Weaver bases. Some shotgun models don't have enough metal along the top of the action to drill and tap for a scope base, so other type mounts must be used.

Gunsmithing supplier Brownells, in Montezuma, Iowa (www.brownells.com), offers four do-it-yourself options for turkey hunters wanting to add a scope to shotguns that are not pre-drilled and tapped. Two of the most popular are the "saddle-type" bases manufactured by B-Square (www.b-square.com) and Aimtech (www.aimtech-mounts.com). My earliest experience with shotgun scope mounts similar to modern saddle mounts was a Weaver detachable fitted for the Remington 870 12 gauge. This early mount was a two-piece affair that incorporated a side plate that attached to the left side of the receiver with two screws that replaced the trigger-group pins. I learned early on that putting too much torque on the mounting screws

will pinch the receiver and cause the bolt to bind when cycling the action. I experienced similar action-binding problems a few years ago, when switching to saddle mounts. To remedy the problem, just back off the tension on the through-receiver screws until the action cycles properly.

Another type of mount you can install yourself is a cantilever rib mount. Remington began producing 870 and 1100 12-gauge slug guns in the early 1990s with cantilever scope mounts. The beauty of these mounts is that they attach directly to the barrel instead of the receiver. Accurately shooting slugs is typically not as good with guns that don't have the barrel rigidly attached to the receiver. Guns such as the Remington 11-87 overcome this weakness by attaching the scope to the barrel via a cantilever. Simply put, a metal bar is screwed to the barrel and extends back over the receiver for normal scope positioning. Remington knew that they had several gun models in the hands

91

of shooters when they brought this new integral scope mounting system to market, so they offered a cantilever scope mount as an after-market add-on that clamps to the vent rib. B-Square also offers a "universal" cantilever rib mount, which will fit ribs up to .380" wide with ½-inch wide vents on 1½-inch center-to-center spacing.

In the cross hairs

Another option is a low-powered scope. A zero-to-3X magnification will work the best. Some scopes have standard cross hairs, while others offer various range-finding reticles. Either diamond-shaped or circular, the center of the reticle covers a specified area, which corresponds to different measurements at different ranges. With practice, you can gauge the range to a gobbler by comparing the reticle's center area to a part of the bird's body, such as the distance from the top of his head to his beard. Pentax, Bushnell, Leupold and Burris scopes have proven top performers on my turkey guns over the years. Pentax probably took the most aggressive approach to the turkey hunting market when they released their 0X-4X variable Lightseeker SG Plus. This scope was created with still-target competition and actual hunting situations in mind.

Whichever scope you choose, make sure that the eye relief is long enough to keep your face away from the rear of the scope. Although I've been lucky, I have seen a few turkey hunters who got too close to their scopes and got some nasty cuts when the scopes came back in recoil.

Over the past few seasons, I've had success with "dot" scopes. I've had equal success with Simmons, Aimpoint and Burris models. It's simple to adjust the cross hairs or dot to cover the center of your shot pattern. It's also easier to keep your gun on target, even in odd shooting positions. A real big advantage is that your sights and your target are in perfect focus at the same time.

Lane Anderson of Blair, Wisconsin wrote:

I am interested in mounting a scope on my Model 9200 Mossberg 12 gauge turkey gun. I have a bad habit of raising my cheek off the stock at the critical moment and shooting over the gobbler's head. I thought a scope might help. In the May/June issue of Turkey Call, the Pentax Lightseeker SG Plus scope was mentioned. What is your opinion of this scope, and will the round reticle help in range estimation? Also, does any company make camo rings and bases to fit my Mossberg 9200?

I replied: You're halfway to solving your problems with missing gobblers if you've determined that you're pulling your face off the stock. Beside helping you concentrate on keeping your face to the stock, a correctly sighted scope will throw a pattern at the center of the cross hairs. The exception would be at very close range. Under ten yards, it will shoot two to three inches low, taking into consideration the height from the muzzle to the scope's cross hairs.

The 2.5X Pentax Lightseeker SG Plus is an ideal scope to mount on your Mossberg. I've used this scope on a Winchester Model 1300 12 gauge turkey gun and found that it has kept its zero after the pounding of several 3-inch magnum loads. NWTF Chairman of the Board Louis Yount has also used the 2.5X Pentax and was happy with its performance.

The circular reticle could be used to judge distances. It represents 7.5 inches for each ten yards. At 40 yards, it encompasses a 30-inch circle; at 50 yards, a 37.5-inch circle. An average mature gobbler is about 36 inches tall when standing erect, and about 33 inches from toenails to the top of the fan when he's in full strut. If the bird is standing erect and fits just inside of the circular reticle, he's at about 50 yards.

Currently, no company makes camouflaged rings and bases to fit a Mossberg 9200. Aimtech Mount Systems and B-Square both make flat black scope mounts that will fit a 9200 Mossberg. Aimtech's address is P.O. Box 223, Thomasville, GA 31799. B-Square's address is P.O. Box 11281, Fort Worth, TX 76110.

17. Getting a Kick Out of Your Turkey Gun

> "Shotguns that kill on one end and wound on the other are definitely reserved for advanced shooters and experienced turkey hunters."

Each summer, the National Wild Turkey Federation hosts a national JAKES weekend at its headquarters in Edgefield, South Carolina. Each year, one of the most popular learning stations has been the patterning station. Each participant is shown some basics of safe gun handling, as well as learning how to pattern a turkey gun.

About five years ago, I recall one twelve-year-old who stood in line and watched several other larger-framed teenagers step up to the bench and take their shots. Many of the older boys had some experience shooting 12-gauge turkey guns and, in a display of testosterone-induced bravado, avoided the wimpy .410s and 20-gauge turkey guns. When the little guy stepped up to the bench for his turn, I already had a .410 single-shot in hand to begin his one-on-one lesson. He confidently informed me that he was going to shoot the 12 gauge instead of the "kid's" gun. I tried to talk him out of his decision, and even asked if his parents would approve his decision. I made a mistake that I have not made since when I reluctantly allowed him to shoulder the Remington 870 and send a 2-ounce turkey load downrange. The tears flowed and he spent the rest of the afternoon with an ice pack on his tender shoulder.

ONE WAY TO COMBAT the effects of recoil is to downsize to a 20 gauge.

That young man's painful experience taught me several lessons, besides the obvious. First, he taught me that no matter what a novice says, their mentor should never subject a young or small-framed shooter to heavy-recoiling turkey loads. At best, it will create a turkey-missing flinch later in the field. At worst, it will turn them off to the idea of shooting and turkey hunting. Second, shotguns that kill on one end and wound on the other are definitely reserved for advanced shooters and experienced turkey hunters.

On the other hand, ample time spent at the range patterning a turkey gun is vital for becoming acquainted with the gun's handling characteristics. Even more important is gaining the faith and confidence that the shotgun and load you will carry into the field are performing at their top potential to make a sure, ethical shot when the moment of truth arrives. Several methods exist for reducing the punishing recoil that often stands in the way of turkey hunters putting enough rounds downrange to become familiar with their turkey guns.

Taming Recoil

Most turkey guns come equipped with a soft recoil pad.

Most factory pads offer some recoil absorption. More advanced recoil-absorbing pads are available from sources such as Brownells' gunsmithing supplies. Ask your local gunsmith for advice on which pad will help absorb more recoil than your factory pad.

Gun weight and action type have a lot of bearing on how much recoil you will feel when you pull the trigger. Lightweight, single-shot and double-barrel guns can be almost unbearable when shooting high-velocity turkey loads. If the gun has a lot of drop in the comb of the stock, the sensation of recoil becomes even greater. Fitting squarely into this category are "youth" 20-gauge single-shots that are chambered for 3-inch loads. If you are introducing a new shooter to the sport, be sure to stick with light field loads during practice sessions. An experienced adult should assist the new hunter by patterning the gun with magnum loads; save the turkey loads until the appropriate time.

You can raise the comfort level a notch by opting for a pump-action shotgun. Simply put, these guns kick less because they are heavier. Their added weight benefits the

shooter by absorbing some of the felt recoil. While patterning your gun, be sure to keep the magazine full, to add a few extra ounces of weight.

After firing thousands of rounds of turkey loads, I prefer testing semi-autos to any other action type. If I have a choice when testing various loads, I'll do my load comparison with a gas-operated 12 gauge. The reason gas-operated or recoil-operated semi-autos kick less is that they bleed off some of the energy supplied from firing the shell into operating the shell-ejection and reloading process. Any energy that gets used up in working the action of the gun doesn't get transferred to your shoulder and cheek.

Other after-market add-on items are recoil-absorbing devices that can be installed inside of the buttstock, as well as the magazine tube. These nifty gizmos work on a principal of hydraulics that helps spread out felt recoil over a longer period, much as the result you get when shooting a gas-operated semi-automatic shotgun.

Form

Shooting form is one of the simplest things that will help

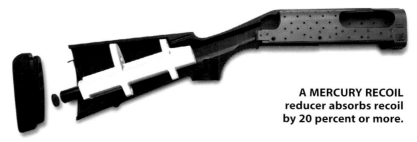

Extra Padding Isn't Just for Show

Past-brand recoil pads are a real help when attempting to tame recoil. These pads are worn over the shirt and put a layer of leather and foam between you and a gun. When I'm shooting, I regularly wear a thinner shotgunning pad under a second, thick rifle pad.

Another trick I learned from experience is to place a small, sand-filled bag between one's shoulder and the gun butt. This will lengthen the effective pull of the stock, but it has not made any difference in accuracy when shooting from a bench. The bag I've been using for years was fashioned from a discarded denim pant leg, a couple of Ziploc bags and a few pounds of dry sand.

you not only shoot more consistently, but feel less recoil. Whenever I am working with children, I emphasize that they mount the gun in their shoulder pocket, instead of lower on their arm. Just as important is how they hold their face to the stock. The mouth should be closed and teeth should be lightly clenched to firm cheek muscles. When the comb of the stock is pressed firmly to the face, it should rest against tight cheek muscles in the same place for each shot. Face surface-area contact with the stock is the key to comfortably "facing" stout-kicking guns. If you try to just lightly press your face to the stock to mentally avoid the inevitable recoil, it allows the gun to pick up momentum at the shot and punch you in the cheek. On the other hand, if you are firmly in contact with the stock, it becomes more of a push, as the weight of your head helps absorb the blow.

Take a Rest

Recoil-absorbing rests have their merits when shooting turkey guns. Several years ago, Zero-coil made a shock-absorbing device that mounted on a shooting bench to arrest recoil. It used heavy springs to tame the backward inertia created by big kickers. GNC Enterprises Recoil Buster debuted its recoil-absorbing device at the 2001 SHOT Show. I got my hands on a model for testing a 10-gauge Remington. I fired a couple of rounds, and first thought that the rest wasn't helping much. I took it off the bench and replaced it with my trusty Outers Varminter Rifle Rest. At the next shot, I knew that the device was definitely worth the trouble of strapping the big 10 in its cradle. I immediately went back to my garage and pulled it back out and finished the day's shooting with the Recoil Buster in place. The way this piece of valuable equipment works is by an internal spring that is attached to a strap. The strap is firmly placed around the butt so that the spring helps absorb the rearward movement of the gun. Although it is somewhat cumbersome, the benefit is worth the trouble.

Give some of these hints a try. Taming recoil will make you a better shooter, which will raise your confidence level in the field next season.

GNC ENTERPRISES' Recoil Buster (P.O. Box 114, Savage, MT 59262) makes range work more enjoyable.

v. Ammo and Its Performance

The first print reference I can find that promotes "turkey loads" appeared in the January 1988 issue of *Turkey Call* in an advertisement for the Activ shotshell company. Its promotional line, "Makes a hull of a difference," was right on the money with the description of their red, brassless 12-gauge hulls. Activ was the first company to offer 3-inch 12 gauge, 2-ounce loads of No. 4 or 6 shot specifically for turkey hunting. During the fall of 1988, Federal Cartridge began marketing magnum 12-gauge loads for turkey hunters. In 1989, Winchester soon followed suit by introduc-ing their Super X turkey loads.

Over the next decade, turkey load development went into high gear as manufacturers raced to perfect loads to meet turkey hunters' performance demands. Federal, Winchester, Remington, and custom loaders all deserve recognition for creating the splendid ammunition available today. The following chapters share a first-hand look at the care that goes into crafting high-performance turkey loads, as well as the individual contributions each manufacturer has made to today's turkey hunting ammunition.

18. Federal Cartridge's Recipe for a Turkey Load

"Out of sight, out of mind," goes the old saying. That old saw certainly applies to most hunters when they consider their turkey loads.

Out of sight, out of mind," goes the old saying. That old saw certainly applies to most hunters when they consider their turkey loads.

I've always been prone to tinker with things, wanting to know what makes them tick. Ever since I was four years old and completely dismantled my tricycle on the front porch, I've been tearing things apart to see how they work.

When I recently got an invitation to tour Federal Cartridge's ammunition plant in Minnesota, I jumped at the chance. *Turkey Call* television field producer, Bob Thompson, and show editor Jason Morrow joined me to take a closer look at what goes into making today's high-performance turkey loads. We followed the process from the raw materials stage all the way to the warehouse. In between, we quickly learned what Federal manufacturing supervisor Mark Hilde specializes in every day: a high degree of product quality control.

FEDERAL CARTRIDGE annually hosts camps to let shotgunning experts test new products.

FEDERAL LOAD'S TURKEY AMMO

The raw components of lead, copper, brass, plastic, powder, and priming chemicals are shipped to Federal's plant where they are run through several simultaneous manufacturing processeses which produce tens of thousands of turkey loads every day.

The basic steps include shot forming, case and primer manufacturing and, finally, loading. At the end of this process, Federal turns a portion of every lot of ammunition over to their laboratory, where loads are tested for consistent velocity, pressure and reliable functioning.

The accompanying photos give an idea of the various steps of production that go into the making of Federal's turkey loads.

Step-by-step Process

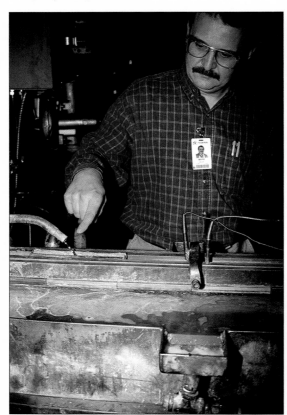

1 Lead ingots, with 7 percent antimony for hardness, are melted in a furnace and the lead is pumped across a sieve that drops the molten metal into a water-cooling bath. The pellets then roll down a wooden baffle, which forms each drop into a round pellet.

2 The pellets roll down a series of ramps that sort out odd-shaped scrap from round pellets. The shot then goes through a series of baffles that sorts them into various sizes. The shot is then plated in a copper and arsenic bath.

3 Plastic pellets are pulled by vacuum into a Reifenhauser, a large machine that melts and extrudes a long, continuous tube that is formed into shell cases.

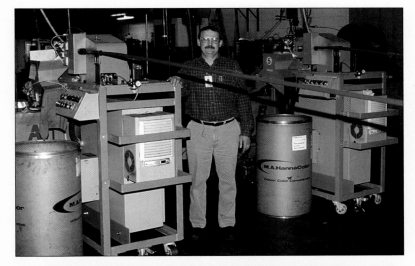

4 Manufacturing supervisor Mark Hilde stands at the end of the Reifenhauser where the shotshell tubes are continuously heated, stretched and finally cut into short tubes.

5 The case heads are stamped from a long sheet of brass, then sent up a long conveyor to another machine that assembles the two components and inserts a primer.

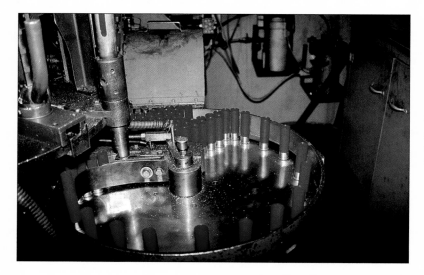

6 The primed turkey load cases are sent to another corner of the plant where they go through the final stages of loading.

7 During the high-speed operation, the cases are filled with powder, followed by a base wad and shot cup. Copper-plated shot is dropped and the shells are crimped.

8 New turkey loads, such as these being packed into NWTF labeled boxes, are packed 10 to a box and cased for shipping. A skilled loader can package 6,000 to 7,000 turkey loads a day.

19. Winchester Turkey Loads

"Winchester was the first company to include a buffering material in lead shotshells, because it dramatically increases pattern density and overall performance of the load."

Winchester's ever-popular turkey loads have gotten even better. In past years, the crimp used on magnum turkey loads allowed a small amount of the Super Grex buffer to leak from the shells, causing a minor loss of effectiveness in patterning.

"Winchester has always looked for ways to make our ammunition better," Mike Jordan, manager of technical services at Winchester Ammunition, said, "even with popular products like our Supreme Double-X Magnum Turkey Load."

Winchester was the first company to include a buffering material in lead shotshells, because it dramatically increases pattern density and overall performance of the load. The improved Double-X load features a new eight-point sealed crimp, which allows the use of a finer shot buffer, resulting in improved patterns and performance.

"Using a finer granulation of Winchester Super Grex buffer improved performance up to 5 percent," Jordan said. "I am sure turkey hunters are going to be even more pleased with the performance of our new Double-X loads."

WINCHESTER historically has taken the lead in turkey load innovations.

Winchester's High-Velocity loads put to the test

In April 1998, there were so many gobbling turkeys surrounding Tim Hooey and me, it was hard to know which way to go. It felt like we were playing musical chairs and having a Chinese fire drill among the endless clumps of mesquite brush in the South Texas pasture. A tom would gobble a couple of hundred yards away, and we'd move again and again to get in a better position to intercept the bird and record it on video for Tim's television show, *North American Fish and Game*.

Finally, we raised the interest of a lone long-beard, and things got hot fast. The mature Rio Grande gobbler came strutting in, but stopped at the 40-yard mark and gobbled for all he was worth. To complicate the matter, a hen popped out from behind another mesquite bush 100 yards away and promised him something we couldn't deliver. When the bird folded his fan and began to walk away, I drew a fine bead with the Mossberg 9200 and lit the fire behind a 1¾-ounce Winchester load of No. 5s.

When I got back to camp, I found 13 pellet holes in the bird's head and neck, none in the breast, and found that four pellets had passed completely through after smashing vertebrae. No wonder he didn't even flop.

I reported on the release of the new Winchester Supreme High-Velocity 1¾-ounce-turkey loads in the May/June 1998 issue of *Turkey Call*. I was pleasantly surprised with their performance at the patterning board. I screwed a Carlson choke tube into the 9200 semi-automatic Mossberg, and it consistently printed patterns around 90 percent at 40 yards. At the time, Winchester decided to only produce these new 3-inch high-velocity loads in No. 5 and No. 6 shot. At the urging of several turkey hunters, Winchester wisely opted to bring out the new 3-inch loads in No. 4 shot as well, early in 1999.

For several years, the emphasis has been on heavier loads for turkeys. In 3-inch 12-gauge magnum rounds, a payload of 2 ounces of shot became the standard. When that much shot gets fired down a 12-gauge barrel, muzzle velocity and downrange energy are sacrificed. These new Winchester 1½-ounce loads come out of a 30-inch test barrel at a blazing 1,300 fps, which is about 15 percent faster than any other 3-inch load on the market.

Adding to the Winchester's High-Velocity turkey loads offered in 1999, Big Red also produced a 3½-inch 12-gauge magnum load stuffed with 2 ounces of No. 4, 5 or 6 shot. Early reports clocked this load at 1,275 fps, which is sizzling for a load of this size. Owners of the Mossberg 835 Ulti-Mag, Browning BPS 3½-inch 12-gauge, and the new Remington 870 Magnum 3½-inch guns were sure to be pleased with the results when they tried this new load.

20. Sport's Newest Turkey Loads Turn Green

"Demand for tungsten-nickel turkey loads drew major attention to an upstart ammunition company."

Today's turkey hunters have access to shotguns that are specifically designed to deliver dense downrange patterns at extended ranges. Since its introduction in January 2000, HEVI•SHOT brand shot has revolutionized the high-performance shotshell market by producing loads that deliver extremely tight pattern density and unmatched downrange pellet energy.

Just ask competitors in the National Wild Turkey Federation World Wild Turkey Still-Target Championships. In 2000, HEVI•SHOT products managed to blow away the competition and beat the existing world record by placing an impressive 42 pellets inside a 3-inch circle at 40 yards. HEVI•SHOT's loads outclassed the competition and took top honors in five major categories at the NWTF competition.

The secret to HEVI•SHOT's superior pattern density and downrange performance is a result of its tungsten-nickel-iron pellet construction. HEVI•SHOT pellets are denser than lead, pellet per pellet, resulting in a seven-percent-heavier pellet that retains more velocity and energy at extended ranges.

Remington Arms Company, Inc., has partnered with ENVIRON-Metal, Inc., to produce Remington Premier HEVI•SHOT Magnum Turkey Loads and Premier High-Velocity HEVI•SHOT Magnum Turkey Loads. In addition, Remington will offer upland and waterfowl HEVI•SHOT loads.

Now turkey hunters can capitalize on the reliability and availability of Remington's shotshell ammunition, while reaping the benefits of HEVI•SHOT pellet performance.

Turkey hunters have been blessed over the past few years by revolutionary advances in shotshell technology. Winchester-Olin first came out with its 12-gauge, 2-ounce Supreme

TUNGSTEN-NICKEL-IRON pellets in Remington's HEVI•SHOT out-performs lead loads.

turkey loads, which far surpassed the pattern performance of earlier loads. Winchester improved their loads by switching from a paper-based wad to a one-piece plastic hull, and adding new components.

When Bob Bryan, former owner of Kick's Choke Tubes, won the 1996 Turkey Shoot with Supreme loads, turkey hunters took notice. Floridian Chuck Smith won the 1997 Turkey Shoot in similar fashion with Winchester Supreme loads.

Turkey ammo technology got another boost in 1998 when Winchester introduced its 1¾-ounce, high-velocity 12-gauge loads. Competitive shooters got on the bandwagon, and Comp-N-Choke's Charlie Boswell won Turkey Shoot titles in 1998 and 1999 with high-velocity Winchester loads.

Over the past few years, ammo manufacturers learned a thing or two after retooling their steel waterfowl loads. The technology transfer is apparent in the performance of today's high-velocity turkey loads.

"The high-velocity turkey loads came about from what we learned from steel loads," said Mike Jordan, Winchester's manager of public relations and public affairs. "Wads, buffer and powders were improved, and formed the basis for the high-velocity turkey loads."

RANDY LEWIS shows his winning form during the NWTF World Wild Turkey Still-Target Championships.

Federal Cartridge stepped up to the plate in 1999 when it appealed to turkey hunters' desire for high-velocity turkey loads. Federal first offered 1¾-ounce, 12-gauge loads in No. 4 and No. 6 shot, and then filled the gap in 2000 with the introduction of its high-velocity 12-gauge loads in No. 5 shot. To say that I'm a fan of the faster-but-lighter turkey loads would be an understatement.

The results of the last two NWTF World Wild Turkey Still-Target Championships may foretell the next chapter in turkey load advancement. Randy Lewis, of Morristown, Tennessee, won the 2000 still-target title with ENVIRON-Metal's HEVI•SHOT, a tungsten-nickel matrix shot that also set a new still-target world record in the 2001 preliminary competition when Claude Kinsler, of Morristown, Tennessee, put 42 pellets inside the 3-inch scoring ring. The actual score would have been higher if the four pellets that cut the outer scoring were included in the final score. The former record was a 34 fired during the 1999 Turkey Shoot.

HEVI•SHOT was initially introduced at the 2000 Shooting, Hunting and Outdoor Trade (SHOT) Show as an alternative non-toxic waterfowl load. Once again, the improvement of waterfowl loads has helped wild turkey loads evolve.

In 1986, I first learned about non-toxic alternatives to steel shot. Over a cup of coffee, Tennessee native John Shannon shared his ideas for everything from polymer-coated lead to using non-precious heavy metals to produce non-toxic shot. Over the next two years, Shannon tried and failed to get his polymer-coated Safety-Shot past the rigors of the U.S. Fish and Wildlife Service approval process. His next step was to switch to a tungsten-iron shot recipe, which he subsequently patented.

By 1989, Shannon had taken on a partner and raised enough venture capital to move his idea forward. At the time, I had recently moved from Memphis, Tennessee, to Marietta, Georgia. After nearly two years working for the *Mid-South Hunting & Fishing News*, I changed jobs and went to work for Game & Fish Publications as the editor of *Arkansas Sportsman*, *Mississippi Game & Fish*, and *Louisiana Game & Fish* magazines. Shannon sent a Safety-Shot company prospectus, hoping to drum up a little promotion and additional capital.

After getting turned down by major ammunition manufacturers, Safety-Shot fell on hard times.

"Safety-Shot ran out of money in 1992, so I failed to renew the patent," Shannon said. Federal Cartridge now owns a patent on tungsten-iron shot.

During the late 1980s and early 1990s, Shannon told me about the exciting possibilities of producing tungsten-based shot for turkey loads.

"Theoretically, tungsten by itself could produce shot that is about 60-percent heavier than lead, so you could fit a three-ounce load in a two-ounce shot cup," Shannon said.

POLYWAD first loaded HEVI•SHOT for ENVIRON-Metal.

Premier HEVI·SHOT Magnum Turkey Load offerings in 2002:				
12 ga.	2½ inch	1³/₈ oz.	# 4, 5, 6	1250 fps
12 ga.	3 inch	1⁵/₈ oz.	# 4, 5, 6	1225 fps
12 ga.	3½ inch	1⁷/₈ oz.	# 4, 5, 6	1225 fps

Premier High Velocity HEVI·SHOT Magnum Turkey Load offerings in 2002:				
12 ga. HV	3 inch	1½ oz.	# 4, 5, 6	1300 fps
12 ga. HV	3½ inch	1½ oz.	# 4, 5, 6	1300 fps

Remington" Premier" Nitro HEVI·SHOT™ offerings for 2002:			
10 ga.	3½ inch	1½ oz.	# 2, 4
12 ga.	2½ inch	1½ oz.	# 4, 6, 7½
12 ga	3 inch	1½ oz.	# 2, 4, 6
12 ga.	3½ inch	1½ oz.	# 2, 4, 6
20 ga.	2½ inch	1⅛ oz.	# 4, 6

Remington "Premier" HEVI·SHOT™ Extra-Long Range			
12 ga.	2½ "	1½ oz.	4, 6, 7½
20 ga.	3 "	1⅛ oz.	4, 6, 7½

Looking deeper into tungsten-based shotshell components reveals some exciting aspects of the heavier-than-lead element. Its hardness resists shot deformation when you pull the trigger, so it has the potential to fly truer than lead shot, which will deform. The hardness also helps penetration, since less energy is wasted to deformation. Tungsten is denser than lead, but equal in weight and smaller in size. Tungsten also has less wind drag and penetrates soft tissue with less resistance. Simply put, it's possible to get a No. 6-size tungsten-nickel matrix shot pellet to weigh as much–hitting as hard and penetrating farther–as a No. 5 lead shot pellet.

"Tungsten is much harder than lead, so you must be careful how you load it," Shannon added. "Hard shot, like steel or tungsten, requires a heavy shot cup, to prevent it from scratching shotgun barrels and destroying chokes."

Over the past several months, I have patterned various tungsten-based waterfowl shotshells manufactured by Federal Cartridge and Kent Cartridge. Both companies have repackaged some of their tungsten waterfowl loads as turkey loads, but they have been slow to catch on among turkey hunters.

As a turkey hunter, I've been hesitant to jump on the tungsten turkey load bandwagon. My limited experience patterning the Federal tungsten-iron and Kent tungsten-matrix ammo was promising, but not good enough to warrant a switch from high-velocity lead turkey loads.

My interest in tungsten-based turkey loads was renewed when I discovered ENVIRON-Metal's HEVI•SHOT waterfowl loads in the new products section of the 2000 SHOT Show. Company owner Daryll Amick's claim that HEVI•SHOT was 11 percent heavier than lead got my undivided attention. The potential existed for turkey load technology to make a significant leap in performance on paper targets and in the field.

One of my first phone calls after returning from the SHOT Show was to Amick. I learned more about his fledgling company and his history in the shooting industry. Ironically, Amick was the metallurgist who created the formula for what is now Federal Cartridge's tungsten-iron and tungsten-polymer waterfowl loads. After he retired, Amick said that he felt that he could further improve tungsten-based shotshell loads.

Curious to learn how this new shot would hold up in competition, I explained to Amick the NWTF's World Wild Turkey Still-Target Championships. Amick's confidence was evident when he soon elected to become a sponsor for the competition. His company went head to head with the other ammunition sponsors, Winchester and Federal, in August 2000 in

Forsyth, Georgia. HEVI•SHOT's win and new world record earned Amick some bragging rights, which has since sparked serious attention from shooters and manufacturers alike.

During range analysis with tungsten-based loads in October 2000, I compared Federal, Kent Cartridge and HEVI•SHOT loads. I disassembled a HEVI•SHOT round from the lot fired in the 2000 NWTF Still-Target competition to examine its contents. I weighed the shot charge and found that it weighed 1½-ounces, rather than the 1⅝-ounces that the loads were reported to weigh. The significance of the fact is that the shot charges were as much as ¼ ounce lighter than the previous winning shotshell but turned in better pattern performance. Another thing I learned was the variation in size of HEVI•SHOT's individual pellets.

One of the manufacturing characteristics of tungsten-nickel shot is that a wide range of shot sizes is produced from a single pour of molten metal. As with lead shot, it must be sorted according to size before loading. To meet Turkey Shoot rules, HEVI•SHOT had to be thoroughly screened and sorted, with no shot smaller than No. 6 making it to final loads. I measured 100 individual pellets from the HEVI•SHOT load and found that roughly 10 percent of the pellets measured .110, which is the size of a No. 6. The average shot size was .121, which is just slightly larger than a No. 5. To put it simply, the pellets of HEVI•SHOT fired in the competition averaged a full shot size larger than the traditional competition shooters' choice of No. 6 shot. The phrase "Less is more" certainly applied.

Jay Menefee, the owner of Polywad, does a portion of the shotshell loading for HEVI•SHOT, and he said, "Retained velocity is the key to HEVI•SHOT's patterning performance. When it slows down, it hits a critical speed where it naturally disperses. I compare it to the way a knuckle ball or curve ball breaks when it nears home plate. It's passing that threshold of decreased velocity that makes the ball drastically change course. When the shot drops below the speed of sound, the dispersion rate increases dramatically. HEVI•SHOT's tungsten-based load has greater density than lead, which makes it retain velocity for a longer period of time."

Patterning with HEVI•SHOT in October 2000 produced promising results. Fired from 40 yards, I averaged 83 percent patterns in a 30-inch circle, including 81 pellets within a 10-inch circle from a MAD Max choke. A Strangler choke tube produced 89 percent patterns, which also averaged 110 pellets within a 10-inch circle. A Comp-N-Choke tube used in the testing averaged putting 87 percent of a load inside 30 inches and 103 pellets within a 10-inch circle.

In early October 2001, I again visited with ENVIRON-Metal's top gun, Daryll Amick. "Business has been far beyond what was dreamed," Amick said. "By next week we will bring online more production capacity to keep up with business. Over the last six months, we have tripled capacity." Amick revealed that his company would be producing a very large amount of shot the following year.

In 2001, to meet demand, HEVI•SHOT was custom-loaded by three companies. "HEVI•SHOT loads bought through our website can be from any of three loaders," Amick said. "The red shells are loaded by Estate Cartridge Company, which is owned by

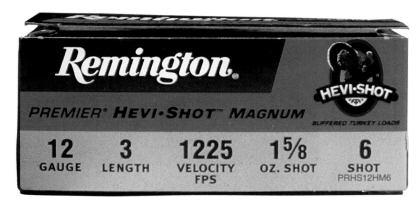

HEVI•SHOT can extend the effective range of most guns by 10 yards or more.

JAY MENEFEE

DUSTY WILLIAMS

NWTF World Wild Turkey Still-Target Championships

When the smell of gunpowder had faded from the firing line at The Meadows National Gun Club, Randy Lewis, of Morristown, Tennessee, placed enough pellets in the 3-inch red circle of a turkey silhouette paper target to win First Place in the 12-Gauge Open finals at the 2001 National Wild Turkey Federation World Wild Turkey Still-Target Championships.

Lewis defended his World Still-Target 12-Gauge Open title and had to defeat a champion to earn it. Lewis faced Dusty Williams, who had already earned the JAKES (Junior) title in the final round of the open competition. Williams, of Dublin, Georgia, had defeated two-time defending champion Brian Townsend of Lithia, Florida, to take that title. Lewis, shooting a Benelli M1, placed 24 pellets in the red circle to win the 12-Gauge Open competition.

Over 1,258 rounds of turkey shot were fired at turkey-silhouetted paper targets from a distance of 40 yards. The shooter with the most pellets inside a 3-inch red circle won each round, and, ultimately, the competition. The competition was split into two divisions, Open and Hunter. Open-division competitors use shotguns and chokes that have been modified specifically for competition, while Hunter-division competitors were restricted to guns and choke tubes that are available commercially and have not been altered for competition.

Kerry Terrell, of Brooklet, Georgia, placed enough pellets in the scoring ring to win First Place in the 12-Gauge Hunter finals. Julie Townsend, of Lithia, Florida, won First Place in the Ladies' 20 Gauge finals. Jay Menefee, of Macon, Georgia, took First Place in the 20-Gauge Open finals. Ammunition sponsors for the 2001 Turkey Shoot were Federal Cartridge Company, HEVI·SHOT, and Winchester-Olin Corporation.

JULIE TOWNSEND

Federal. The black shells are loaded by Remington, and the clear shells are loaded by Polywad."

The differences between the red, black and clear loads are minimal when it comes to results, but nonetheless important. Polywad loads are created with Italian-made Gualandi wads, and use a spherical shot buffer. The other companies are using standard steel-shot wads and white, crumb-like polyethylene buffer. A major difference between today's loads and early HEVI•SHOT loads is the buffer. Amick said the buffer lowers barrel pressure and improves pattern performance. The HEVI•SHOT-produced turkey loads are 1⅜ ounces and loaded in a 2½-inch hull with a roll crimp, which makes them look like a 3-inch shell. The Estate shells, which have a 1½-ounce load, are loaded in a true 3-inch hull and sealed with a star crimp. "When we went to Estate, we dropped the loads by ⅛ ounce and velocities went to 1,225 fps," Amick said. "I remember what you (the author) told me was a good measure for comparing turkey load performance, a 12 gauge putting 100 pellets in a 10-inch circle at 40 yards," Amick said. "We started loading a 20-gauge shell prior to the 2001 Turkey Shoot, and we were consistently putting 100 to 110 pellets in a 10-inch circle at 40 yards."

When the Turkey Shoot rolled around, HEVI•SHOT was ready to enter the 20-gauge division. "That little shell never lost a preliminary round," Amick said. "The champion wound up being good old Jay Menefee."

"It's going to take us a while to convert people to shooting smaller shot sizes," Amick said. "The rigidity with the density (of the shot) is something people are not used to yet."

"HEVI•SHOT lives up to its name and reputation," said Remington press relations manager Eddie Stevenson. HEVI•SHOT's trademarked slogan, "Heavier than lead. Not a lead substitute, a lead improvement" is evidenced through pattern density and penetration tests, as well as performance on game. Stevenson reported that penetration tests were conducted by shooting Remington HEVI•SHOT No. 4 loads at 24-gauge-thick galvanized steel at 40 yards. In comparison, No. 4 lead loads dented the steel while the HEVI•SHOT No. 4s passed clear through it.

It should be mentioned that extreme caution should be taken when shooting HEVI•SHOT at hard surfaces. During the NWTF Still-Target competitions, it was reported that the HEVI•SHOT was striking the steel target holders and bouncing back to the firing line. Protective eyewear should always be worn when shooting these or any other loads.

Remington's turkey loads were made available to hunters on January 1, 2002. All loads are packaged in 10-round boxes.

Stevenson also reported that the Remington HEVI•SHOT loads, when shot through a modified choke, were placing about 20 percent more pellets on target than conventional lead loads at 40 yards. The difference when comparing steel-shot loads was even more impressive. HEVI•SHOT loads were putting approximately 49 percent more pellets on target than comparative No. 4 steel loads.

Remington ballisticians are also busy learning the best choke constrictions for use with HEVI•SHOT. "The magic constriction is between full and super-full," Stevenson said. All testing was conducted with a standard Rem-Choke barrel, which measures .725. A Remington full choke measures .687, while a super-full turkey choke measures .665.

Remington offers its HEVI•SHOT loads to waterfowl hunters in 10, 12, and 20 gauge magnum with 2¾, 3, and 3½-inch shells available in 12-gauge. HEVI•SHOT is available in 10-gauge 3½-inch magnum and 20-gauge 3-inch magnum loads. All this offers more options in ammunition to both turkey and waterfowl hunters. Remington also makes long-range tungsten shells for upland game hunters.

21. *Custom Turkey Loads*

NITRO PRESIDENT Raymond Filogomo bagged this 22 ½ pound gobbler with one of his own 12-gauge turkey loads.

In 1995, I received a letter from *Turkey Call* reader George Patenotte, from Paducah, Kentucky, asking for information about a little-known shotshell manufacturer from Gilboa, New York. George wanted to know about the quality of the Nitro Company's various turkey loads in both 10 and 12 gauge.

At the time, the only thing I knew for certain was that fellow turkey hunting scribe Jim Casada was a fan of Nitro's 2½-ounce duplex load of No. 5 x 7½, loaded in 12 gauge hulls. Prompted by the letter from Mr. Patenotte, I contacted Ray Filogomo, owner of Nitro, to learn more about his specialty shotshells. A few days later, a selection of 10- and 12-gauge loads arrived. Over the course of the next several weeks I was pleasantly surprised by my test results with them.

Using a Remington SP-10 semi-auto to try the 3½-inch 10-gauge magnum loads, I found the 2½- and 3-ounce No. 5 x 7½ loads threw center-dense patterns at 40 yards. Not surprisingly, the SP-10 showed a preference at the patterning board, with the 2¼-ounce load coming out on top by a wide margin. This awesome load averaged 87-percent patterns inside a 30-inch circle at 40 yards, with 40 pellets striking the head-and-neck area on a Winchester-Olin patterning target.

Stepping up to the heavier loads, the patterns opened up considerably. The 2½-ounce load of No. 5 x 7½ shot printed 47 percent patterns, and placed 20 pellets in the head-and-neck area.

The 3-ounce loads averaged 45 percent inside

NITRO AMMUNITION squeezes out more performance from most turkey guns.

the standard 30-inch patterning rings, with 29 hits in the vitals. The two heavier loads opened up to improved-cylinder ratings, which tells me that these loads are a tad overmatched for the Remington factory extra-full tube. Aside from the benefit of lighter recoil generated by the 2¼-ounce loads, their devastating patterns promised to spell trouble for any lusty tom that ventured into range during the next season.

A chance to put these Nitro loads to the ultimate test came in mid-April when I located a pair of gobblers strutting in a clearcut just five minutes away from my home in Edgefield, South Carolina. The first morning, the gobbling duo had traveling on their minds as they strutted by my setup spot, never coming closer than 80 yards. The next morning, I set up close to their roost, only

to have them fly down in the other direction and follow the same course as the previous morning. I noted their travel route and made plans to change my tactics the third morning.

On day three, I guessed that I would have two chances to intercept the travelers as they skirted close to two wooded points where mature timber jutted out into the clearcut. When they were nearly within range of my first setup, a trio of jakes diverted the mature birds' attention. They chased the youngsters away from the "hen" they had been propositioning. Continuing their course of the previous two days, the two longbeards walked away, preferring to let the hen they heard come to them instead of the way I had planned.

The birds safely out of sight, I got up and jogged 600 yards through the woods to cut them off. Much to my chagrin, I spied the longbeards walking past just as I slid into position. A few yelps served to stop the longbeards, but they were content to strut and wait for the hen to come to them. We kept up a conversation for the next 15 minutes, but the toms wouldn't come any closer than 90 yards. As luck would have it, the jakes strolled by me and started looking for companionship. I started cutting and purring on a mouth call, and it was more than the jealous longbeards could stand. They moved in to run the jakes off again, and strutted closer. At 10 yards, one tom poked his head

around a sweet gum sapling and caught a faceful. Neither the turkey nor the tree fared well. It was rewarding and awe-inspiring to bag a bird that I had worked for three hunts, and to watch a tree 2 inches in diameter topple over, from a single pull of the trigger.

Another Nitro offering I tested was a 12-gauge, 2½-ounce, 3-inch magnum load of No. 5 x 7½ shot. Fired from a Remington 11-87 semi-auto with a factory choke tube measuring .665, this load printed 74-percent patterns with an average of 31 pellet strikes in the head and neck printed on the Winchester patterning targets. I fired the same load from my old favorite, a Remington Sportsman 12 that has had quite a bit of modification. With an ultratight .640 tube in place, the same load opened up to produce 51-percent patterns at 40 yards with 15 pellets in the vitals.

Again, too much choke constriction opened up patterns with the hot-and-heavy Nitro loads in the guns I used for testing. Nitro offers 10 different buffered loads for 3½-inch 10 gauge, 3½-, 3- and 2½-inch 12 gauge. They load single shot sizes in No. 4 and No. 7½, four duplex loads, and two triplex loads: 4 x 5 x 7½-and 2 x 4 x 7½. Velocities for all loads range between 1,100 and 1,200 feet per second.

For more information, call (417) 746-4600, or write to 7560 Newkirk Road, Mountain Grove, MO 65711.

VI. Smokepoles and Sharp Sticks

After several seasons pursuing wild turkeys and putting several tags on cooperative gobblers, many hunters search for ways to challenge themselves. The handicap presented by going afield with a black powder shotgun or a bow heightens the hunting experience and raises satisfaction when we score. The next couple of chapters share some of my experiences, both good and bad, while hunting with charcoal burners or sticks and strings. Check out some of the handy tips to up your chances for success, too.

22. Muzzleloaders for Turkey Hunting

"The MK-86 killed every 'paper' tom."

MODERN Muzzleloading's founder Tony Knight is an avid turkey hunter.

Squirrels are traitors! When I first recorded this in my hunting journal, about three weeks had passed since the Missouri turkey season closed, and it took an appreciable amount of time to come up with a printable invective to describe these vermin. If you're wondering what caused my venomous attitude, I'll be glad to explain.

I had been invited by gunsmith-inventor Tony Knight to join a few other hunting writers for a chance to try out Modern Muzzleloading's new MK-86 12-gauge black powder shotgun on an Iowa gobbler. The spring foliage in 1995 was behind schedule and the turkeys were, too. It made for some frustrating hunting conditions. I could hear as many as eight mature birds gobbling while I stood in one spot every morning.

On the fourth morning, I set up on a logged-off point of a ridge, about 90 yards from a pair of birds roosted along a creek, two toms I had roosted the evening before. I was between them and a cornfield they had strutted in the previous morning. A little tree talk got the gobblers cranked up, so I just sat back and listened for them to fly down. After I heard them fly down, they went silent, refusing to answer my calls.

Forty-five minutes passed as I waited for the birds to give me an indication of their location, so I could make my next move. Suddenly, I heard heavy footfalls bounding up the ridge behind me. My instincts shouted that a turkey was trotting up the back side of the ridge and I had better get into position fast. I leaned left around the big oak I was sitting against and swung the scope-sighted muzzleloader into position. I locked the cross hairs on the most likely opening, between two vine-covered piles of oak tops, and waited for the bird to step into view. Thumb on the safety, I was still as stone waiting for the bird to walk into my line of fire.

What happened next is the reason for my contempt of all rodents who live in trees. A ponderous orange fox squirrel crawled out of the oak top and hopped to the ground mere feet from me, and began to dig about in the leaves for his breakfast. I figured this was the source of the noise that had put me on alert. The wretched rodent's decoying trick worked, fooling me into lowering my guard—and my gun. No sooner had I raised my cheek off the stock than a fine longbeard stepped around a tree a mere 20 feet away, and immediately went airborne. As the bird pumped for altitude, I proceeded to shoot where the bird wasn't.

After rising to my feet and getting the kinks out, I recharged the front-stuffer and tried to recall if Iowa was one of the states with a spring squirrel season.

Although I didn't connect on that hunt, a few others did. Famous outdoors writer Gary Clancy, *Turkey & Turkey Hunting* contributing editor Jim Casada, Toby Bridges, and Tony Knight got the job done with their MK-86 shotguns.

It wasn't until I got the gun back home and got a chance to do some serious range work that I really caught on to what this new-generation muzzleloading shotgun was capable of producing. I was firm in the belief that 30 yards was the absolute maximum for any scattergun burning black powder or its equivalent. Short-range shots seemed to go along with the other self-imposed limitations inherent with muzzleloading for turkeys. After spending a couple of days at the shooting range, I realized that not having a quick second shot was the only thing I'd be giving up with this gun.

What I found was that the MK-86 consistently produced murderous patterns at the 40-yard mark, and killed every paper tom shot at from the 50-yard line.

The secret to the tight patterns is Modern Muzzleloading's extended screw-in choke tubes, identical to the types available for practically every smokeless powder turkey gun on the market today. These choke tubes are so tight (.660-inch for the one supplied with the gun I used for testing) that they have to be removed when loading the weapon.

Most of the MK-86 12-gauge guns seem to favor 100 to 120 grains of RS Pyrodex behind a

Where to Find It

Knight Rifles
21852 Hwy. J46
Centerville, IA 52544
www.knightrifles.com

Oehler Chronographs
Oehler Research
P.O. Box 9135
Austin, TX 78766
www.oehler-research.com

Pyrodex
Hodgdon Powder Co.
P.O. Box 2932
Shawnee Mission, KS 66201
www.pyrodex.com

CCI/Speer-Blount, Inc.
2299 Snake River Ave.
Lewiston, ID 83501
www.cci-ammunition.com

Winchester Reloading
Components
Olin/Winchester
427 North Shamrock St.
East Alton, IL 62024-1174
www.winchester.com

KNIGHT'S MK-86 Convertible 12 gauge shotgun.

PYRODEX, modern wads and copper-plated shot give muzzleloaders greater performance.

Winchester AA 1⅛-ounce shotshell wad filled with 1⅝-ounces of No. 5 Winchester-Olin lead shot. This load is topped off with a foam over-wad to keep everything in place.

My favorite load leans toward the heavier powder charge, which consistently produced even patterns that put an average of 75.5 percent of the pellets in a 30-inch circle at 40 yards. Also, at this extended range the MK-86 kept putting 10 to 15 of the No. 5 pellets into the head and neck of Winchester's large turkey patterning targets. Another quality I noticed about the shot patterns was the even distribution of the shot. Within that 30-inch circle at 40 yards, a gobbler will likely contract an immediately-terminal case of lead poisoning.

Putting holes in paper never tells the whole story of what will happen when you trip the trigger on a game animal. To get a better idea, I chronographed several loads to see if they had enough velocity–and subsequent foot pounds of striking energy–to give the penetration needed for quick, clean kills. I set up an Oehler chronograph and sent several 1⅛-ounce loads downrange. The load powered with 120 grains of RS Pyrodex produced an average of 1,221 fps for ten shots with the chronograph's skyscreens set up 3 feet from the muzzle. This load is on par with many 2¾-inch magnum 12-gauge loads.

I made a call to Mike Jordan and Bob Miklos at Winchester-Olin to pick their brains on what this load was doing at the 40-yard mark. A No. 5 shot that starts out at 1,221 fps will slow to 713 fps at 40 yards, and will yield 2.9-foot pounds of energy on impact. If memory serves, a minimum of six pellet strikes in a turkey's head and neck with 2.4 foot pounds of energy per pellet is required to provide enough penetration for a clean kill.

The MK-86 shotgun is on par with the better smokeless-powder turkey guns on the market today. It will do anything a repeater can do on turkeys, except give quick second shots.

A noticeable benefit of carrying the MK-86 is its light weight. The MK-86's 7 pounds, with a 1-3x Weaver scope attached, is a pleasure to lug around all day. A bonus for the MK-86 shooter will be accessory barrels in .50 and .54 caliber. This gun has a removable barrel, which allows for easy cleaning, or switching from a smoothbore to a rifled barrel.

Knight's TK-2000

Regrettably, Modern Muzzleloading has discontinued manufacturing the MK-86. Tony Knight invented another shotgun to take its place. The TK-2000 is a fixed-barrel 12-gauge shotgun that accepts screw-in chokes. This newer model has performed to the same standards on paper and in the field as the MK-86.

23. The Bowhunter's Challenge

"An unusual audience gives a memorable twist to a mixed-bag challenge for whitetails and wild turkeys during the Buckeye State's first fall turkey season."

The following story began as an Ohio deer hunt, but it quickly turned into a spectacular fall turkey hunt.

The Spectator

Sitting atop a deer stand among the swaying limbs of a red oak, I barely heard my own thoughts. The blue skies and blustery conditions had deer movement down to a minimum during daylight hours, so I had plenty of time to rest after spending two days combing several southeastern Ohio ridges in search of a wild turkey for Thanksgiving dinner.

From all indications, the Ohio Department of Wildlife Conservation's opening of a limited fall turkey season in several counties was well timed. Over the past 48 hours, I had counted at least 15 different birds that, for one reason or another, had just barely managed to elude my efforts to punch my tag. My thoughts drifted back to a flock of seven long-bearded gobblers that had approached my calling from behind. They had never uttered a yelp. Only their footfalls in the leaves announced their presence. Several tense moments had passed as the birds milled around, looking for the source of calling. Their curiosity satisfied, they left without presenting a decent shot for my 12

THE AUTHOR'S long-time hunting partner, Andy Turner, glasses for toms.

gauge. Other setups during the morning produced little more than occasional distant yelps from birds content to answer, but that came no closer.

That evening, I traded my shotgun for a bow and climbed into a stand overlooking a promising spot where my host had seen a wide-racked buck only days before. As the sun dropped below the horizon, a twist of fate put me within 40 yards of five hens that decided to roost in a nearby sycamore. The conditions were prime for a close encounter the next morning, if everything worked out right.

When it was time to climb down, I lowered my bow to the ground and slipped toward the white-barked sycamore. I whooped and hollered to flush the birds from their roost, sending them in all directions. I marked the direction two of the birds took and made a mental note for the next morning's hunt.

An hour before daylight the next morning, I sat listening to the rain pounding the roof of the truck. The temperature was in the upper 50s, so I decided to don my rain suit and brave the elements. Nearing the area where one of the birds had headed, I stopped and listened between wind gusts.

Faintly at first, I heard a lost hen yelping from its perch. Quickly sitting down, I began to call with a mouth call–the only call I could operate in the downpour. Suddenly, I picked out the form of a flying turkey

sailing down the hollow in my general direction. When the big bird reached a narrow opening in the canopy, it banked hard right and wove its way through the limbs like a wood duck in the timber. I was unprepared when the turkey landed practically at my feet, and the startling encounter at clubbing distance only persuaded the hen to leave as fast as she had come.

Staying put, I began to call immediately. The old boss hen answered from the ridge above, along with another hen, but they regrouped 90 yards from the setup spot and headed for West Virginia. After an hour and a half of bone-soaking, wind-driven rain, a stool at the local coffee shop seemed more hospitable than another moment in the woods.

As I sat daydreaming about the muffed opportunities, my attention was snapped back to the present. A basket-racked 6-pointer stepped into view a mere 15 yards away and walked down the trail toward my tree. Reaching forward, I gingerly picked up my Golden Eagle compound and released the setscrew on my pendulum sight. Coming to full draw, I settled the pin on the buck's brisket, allowing for the animal's tendency to "jump string" at the sound of a close-range bow. When he stopped broadside at 9 yards, I squeezed the trigger on the release and watched as the arrow flew just under the buck's chest. The angle of the shot was so steep that when

the buck dropped down to make his first lunge, he snapped off the arrow shaft, which was sticking in the ground beneath him.

I grunted at the fleeing animal and he stopped behind a screen of brush to investigate what had spooked him. For the next 25 minutes the buck hung around, but never offered another open shot. When the deer finally left, I shook my head in disbelief. How could I have missed such a simple shot?

It was about this time that I got the sensation that I wasn't alone. When I glanced around to see if another deer was approaching from behind me, I came eye to eye with a huge groundhog perched in a dogwood tree 8 yards from my stand. Stretched out on a limb, his big, furry butt wedged against the trunk, he lay there with a glazed, unblinking stare that seemed to mock my poor luck. We sat there, locked in a staring match, me wondering who would blink first. I lost. Adding insult to injury, he yawned and stretched and went to sleep. I imagined he was thinking, "If this goof can't hit a big old deer at that range, I don't have a thing to worry about."

Over the next 45 minutes, I amused myself by taking my old Ranging rangefinder and marking the distance to all the trees around my stand inside 70 yards–twice. When I was dialing in the distance on the same white oak for the third time, I heard footsteps approaching from down the hill along the fence. One, then two, then seven more hens fed into bow range. I was pinned down, knowing that any one of the 18 eyes would spot me the second I drew my bow and the game would be over. Several of the birds became interested in acorns lying beneath the limbs of a freshly fallen treetop. One lone hen earnestly scratched at the base of a tree I had marked at 25 yards. All of the birds' heads were out of sight, so I came to full draw and put the pin on the hen's wing butt. A perfect release, and the arrow flew and stuck right at the bird's feet, sending it hopping into the air. I eased my hand to my quiver, strapped to the tree, and glanced at the arrows to get a reload. I couldn't help looking over at the spectating groundhog, whose taunting glare seemed to say, "Go ahead, try it again, you don't have anything else to do."

Moving like molasses in January, I finally got another arrow on the string and tried to pick out another turkey. The flock moved off a few

yards to the left at the first shot, but one straggler once again became interested in scratching for acorns. The bird was at 30 yards, the maximum range for the pendulum sight. After a summer of practicing in my backyard from this range, if I concentrated I could keep all my shots in a group the size of a coffee cup at that distance. When the moment was right, I drew and placed the pin on the hen's backbone as it faced away from me. The arrow flew straight, but seemed to dip too early, again sticking in the ground at the bird's feet. It hopped into the air like it had been rudely goosed and trotted off a few yards.

All the commotion convinced the flock to look for acorns elsewhere. I reached for another arrow and realized that I was down to my last chance. I looked over at the groundhog, spectator of the great archery fiasco. I couldn't tell if he was disgusted or bored with my performance.

Then, I remembered that I had a diaphragm call in my shirt pocket. I fished it out, popped it

BAGGING a wild turkey with a bow is a supreme challenge.

118

struck bird falter and go down 70 yards away.

Climbing down, I walked over to the hen and admired my first bow-killed wild turkey. After tagging the 12-pound hen, I got busy locating arrows, since I was out of ammo and still had 50 minutes for a chance at another deer. When I climbed back aboard the tree stand, I looked over at The Spectator. If this varmint was capable of conscious thought, he was probably muttering something about the luck of blind hogs and acorns. In my defense, I began examining my sight and found that the pendulum pin had worked its way loose and had moved out of its proper position. From that point on, I vowed to shoot a sighter arrow every time I got on stand, to make sure my sights were still in tune (I stuck to my self-imposed promise, and a few weeks later at Tara/Willow Point, I tagged a handsome 9-pointer).

Nothing else stirred that evening. When it was quitting time, I packed up my gear to lower it to the ground. As I was easing my bow down, The Spectator climbed down from his limb and shuffled off down the hill to his den.

Gear in hand, I slung my prize over my shoulder for the half-mile walk out. The weight of the bird was pleasant. I smiled as I felt that faint, rhythmic thumping of feather on fabric, timed with each step. My smile grew wider, reflecting on an autumn day I'll never forget, spent on an Ohio ridge with The Spectator.

Realtree Inventor Shares Passion for Turkey Hunting

Keeping in step with white-tailed deer restoration, the popularity of bowhunting for deer has taken a quantum leap over the past three decades. Today, the combination of healthy wild turkey populations in every state except Alaska, and the tremendous number of bowhunters, has led to an increase in the number of archers who pursue wild turkeys.

Even though bowhunting for turkeys has taken off, few specialized pieces of equipment have been introduced to meet the needs of bowhunters in pursuit of winged big game. Largely, archery manufacturers meet the needs of bowhunters, who pursue wild turkeys with

into my mouth, and gave my best hen yelps and aggravated purrs–the aggravation being quite personal. The lead hen answered from just out of sight. In a moment, the whole troupe came trotting, in a line, back toward my tree. I reached my right hand forward and locked down the setscrew on the cursed pendulum sight. This time I would trust my shooting to some old-fashioned fixed pins. The birds quickly closed the gap–50, 40, 30 yards. When the boss hen went behind a tree, I drew and held the 20-yard pin just to the side of the red oak tree that was 19 yards distant. She came around it leading the flock, but she saw me when she cleared the cover of the tree trunk. I tried to get the pin on her, but she was already briskly walking away. The second bird in line made the fatal mistake of watching the boss hen instead of the danger from above. I switched targets and punched the trigger when the pin came to rest on the second hen's chest. The 125-grain Thunderhead sliced through the bird's vitals, coming to rest a few feet behind her. The flock beat a hasty retreat as I watched the mortally

Bill Jordan's Bowhunting Tips

Bill Jordan has enjoyed a high success rate when bowhunting for wild turkeys because he follows a simple set of strategies. A primary credo Jordan follows is to only shoot when a very high-percentage shot presents itself. "I'd rather let a turkey or deer go than wound one," Jordan said. "Make sure that you put everything in your favor. Where it's marginal, it's better to let a bird go, and go find and set up on another gobbler. It's not so much that I'm a great shot with a bow; I only take very high-percentage shots."

One of the major obstacles in bowhunting for wild turkeys is being caught in the act of drawing your bow when a bird is at close range. Special precautions developed through years of experience by successful bowmen like Jordan will up your chances of bagging a sharp-eyed turkey with your bow.

Jordan's other tips are good advice for any turkey hunter wishing to try bowhunting for these elusive creatures:

1. Learn turkey anatomy. "You owe it to the game to be the best you can be," Jordan says. Shoot for the vitals. Arrow placement should be for the rather small heart-and-lung area or the spine.

2. "Become comfortable shooting from a sitting position," he adds. Jordan uses a small, simple stool that is nothing more that a compact seat and a monopod leg. These seats are manufactured by Preston Pittman Game Calls. He also advises archers to practice shooting from sitting or kneeling positions as much as possible.

3. Get behind cover. "Set up behind a tree, rather than in front of it, when bowhunting for turkeys," Jordan says. "Everyone has been taught to sit in front of a tree when calling a gobbler, but to be successful with a bow, you've got to learn to set up and shoot from behind cover."

4. Use a second caller. "It helps to hunt with a partner, so the second person can keep calling to divert the gobbler's attention when he gets close. It helps a lot that our cameramen are turkey hunters. After I get a bird coming, they start calling when the bird is close to bow range, and it throws the bird off. If the bird is not looking for me, it's much easier to draw undetected."

5. Be confident in your equipment. "I believe that you have to be comfortable with your bow and, again, take high-percentage shots. Hunt turkeys with the bow that you deer hunt with."

6. Limit your range. "Don't shoot beyond the distance you're comfortable shooting accurately. I limit my shots to 30 yards or less."

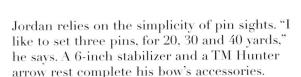

NAP AND other companies' expandable broadheads fly like field points.

the same equipment offered to deer hunters. Fortunately, the lack of specialized equipment hasn't hampered enthusiasm for taking birds with archery tackle.

One famous bowhunter who has carried his zeal for hunting antlered game to that of wild turkeys is Realtree Camouflage inventor Bill Jordan. His practical approach to archery equipment for turkey hunting should encourage other archers to give this challenging facet of the sport a try.

When asked why he started bowhunting for turkeys, Jordan replied, "More than anything else, it was the added challenge" of hunting with primitive weapons. Over the past several seasons, Jordan has killed 18 gobblers with a bow. He averaged two or three birds each year until 1995, when he added the personal challenge of taking a turkey hunter's Grand Slam while being on camera, an added handicap. He was successful, taking an Eastern, Florida, Merriam's and two Rio Grande turkeys. These hunts were combined with others on the Realtree video, All Stars of Spring III.

When it comes to picking archery equipment for turkey hunting, Jordan takes a practical approach by sticking with the same setup he uses for deer.

Jordan's choice of draw length fits a distinct style of bowhunting. "I always shoot from a sitting position while hunting from a tree stand for deer or sitting on the ground for turkeys," he noted. A bow with a 30-inch draw would fit him perfectly, but Jordan opts instead for a 28½-inch draw length, which is more comfortable for him to shoot from a sitting position. "I shoot a mechanical release, and like to feel it bottom out when I draw, so the shorter length feels more comfortable," he said.

Jordan's choice of a 75-pound draw-weight bow offers an advantage. "At 75 pounds, an arrow has a flatter trajectory than less draw-weights," he says. The most important part of selecting a draw-weight for turkey or deer hunting is a poundage that you can hold comfortably for at least 60 seconds."

Still, after 29 years of bowhunting,

Jordan relies on the simplicity of pin sights. "I like to set three pins, for 20, 30 and 40 yards," he says. A 6-inch stabilizer and a TM Hunter arrow rest complete his bow's accessories.

When it comes to the business end of his archery tackle, Jordan chooses an Easton XX75 2413 shaft, cut to 29½ inches, and fletched with the cock vane down. He tips his arrows with a Game Tracker TriLock chisel-point broadhead weighing 125 grains. "I was shooting 100-grain Game Tracker when I took a Grand Slam, but I've since switched to the heavier broadheads. I like these broadheads because they shoot well and fly like field points."

Archery Tackle for Turkeys

During the past few years, a smattering of new archery equipment has been developed for turkey hunting. Primarily, broadheads have been modified for hunting the big birds. Wasp broadheads have a four-blade head with two of the blades modified to create hooks that slow penetration.

New Archery Products (NAP) offers the Spitfire 100 Gobbler Getter broadhead. This 100-grain head is a scissor-type that opens on impact. It has three blades that open to a 1½-inch cutting diameter. This broadhead also incorporates a bullet-style tip that retards penetration.

Some bowhunters opt for string trackers for turkey hunting, since the birds often leave almost no evidence of being hit, or a blood trail. Game Tracker and other manufacturers offer string trackers, which some archers find useful for locating birds after they are hit.

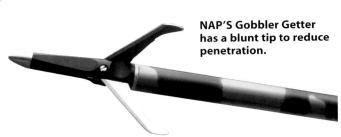

NAP'S Gobbler Getter has a blunt tip to reduce penetration.

VII. *Parting Shots*

Turkey hunters often face equipment problems when traveling afar. A broken sight or other mishaps can ruin a trip if you don't make adequate preparation. Try some of these tips to remedy or avoid unforeseen problems.

24. Field Care and Travel Tips

More than any other group of hunters, turkey hunters have become more mobile in their pursuit of this prized game bird. Traveling with guns takes some special precautions to assure that turkey hunting adventures don't become misadventures. Some of the following tips could save an otherwise disappointing trip.

1. **Carry an extra clamp-on or magnetic sight.** Some of the sights used on today's turkey guns, whether they are rifle-type or telescopic sights, are inherently weaker than a standard bead sight. Sights and their mounts can be damaged or lost in transit or in the field. Having a spare handy to replace faulty sights can save a hunt. Be sure to fire a couple of test shots with the spare sights before hunting to confirm that your turkey loads are hitting point of aim.

2. **Carry a compact cleaning kit.** While a mishap resulting from a clogged barrel presents a safety hazard, failure to clean the barrel will harm pattern effectiveness. A three-piece cleaning rod can be a hunt-saver. A veteran turkey hunter told me that more than once he has loaned his cleaning

A COLLAPSIBLE cleaning kit helps clear debris from a clogged bore.

rod to companion hunters. Firing a magnum turkey load through a dirty chamber is a recipe for sticky extraction. If the case sticks firmly enough, the extractor will pull through the case rim and leave the hull hopelessly stuck.

3. **Some traveling turkey hunters** opt for packing their valued guns in a metal gun case fitted with a crossbar, locked down with a padlock. These cases are worth the added expense, since they will outlast lower-priced hard plastic models.

4. **When packing a shotgun** in an airline-approved hard case, first place the gun in a padded soft gun case to add some extra protection.

5. **Pack your gun with the bottom** of the gun toward your hard gun case's hinge. If a careless baggage handler drops the case and the gun slides to the bottom of the case, the sights won't

strike the hinge's hard surface. Experience taught me this one. On one trip several years ago, my gun case was dropped so hard that it severely dented the hinge, which in turn bent an 870 Remington's vent-ribbed barrel and knocked off the mid-bead.

6. **If you are going to fly,** consider shipping your guns ahead via UPS or Federal Express to a licensed gun dealer in the area in which you will be hunting. That way you won't face the problem of arriving at your destination without your gun.

7. **When you arrive at your hunting location,** pattern your gun to be sure that it still strikes at your point of aim. In addition to checking to be sure your sights haven't been knocked out of alignment, it will assure that a possible change in altitude between where you originally patterned

PACK YOUR GUN in a soft case inside a hard case to give added protection when traveling by air.

your gun and your new location are similar. For instance, a gun patterned at sea level and carried to a higher altitude will tend to shoot tighter in less-dense mountain air. The opposite is true for guns taken from high elevations to sea level.

8. **Include a small tool kit in your gun case.** A multiplier and a small set of Allen wrenches will come in handy if something shakes lose in transit.

9. **Sling your gun.** If your turkey gun isn't equipped with a carrying sling, consider adding one, or get one of the leather models that cinches over the barrel and butt stock grip. Most of the turkey hunters I know spend a much larger percentage of their time carrying a shotgun than shooting it. Your arms will

be less fatigued at the end of the day.

10. **When taking a commercial airline flight,** tape up your gun case latches to keep them from becoming snagged, but wait until after you fill out a firearms certification card.

11. **It's a good idea to attach a laminated card** with your name and address to the outside of your gun case when traveling on a commercial airline. An added precaution is to include your name and address inside the case as a backup. If your luggage tags and baggage claim tags are accidentally removed, the airline still has a means to identify your equipment.

12. **If your turkey gun can be broken down** and the barrel removed, consider a compact gun case that will be easier to handle in busy airports and take up less space in general. One of my favorites is a Doscocil case that measures 38 inches by 12 inches and is 4 inches thick. In a pinch, as many as two shotguns with the barrels removed can fit in this case. This can be a plus if you are traveling with a friend, in light of most airlines' restrictions on the number of bags travelers can check.

13. **If you pack your gun in a hard gun case** for airline travel, include a lightweight gun sock in your gear. Some states require that guns be cased when in a vehicle, and a gun sock is much easier to use when taking a shotgun in and out of a vehicle.

14. **A good practice to follow** with all your firearms is to photograph them and keep a record of their serial numbers. If a gun is stolen, or lost by an airline, a photo is handy for identification or justification of its value.

15. **Keep gun cases and guns out of sight when possible.** Locked hotel rooms are a safer bet than securing them in a vehicle. It only takes seconds to break a window, pop a trunk, or open an unlocked door. I know of several people who have had their prized guns stolen from their vehicles.

Index

Picture Credits